PROFESSION OF FAITH OF
A SAVOYARD VICAR

BY
J. J. ROUSSEAU

WILDSIDE PRESS

www.wildsidepress.com

INTRODUCTION

ABOUT thirty years ago a young man, who had forsaken his own country and rambled into Italy, found himself reduced to a condition of great poverty and distress. He had been bred a Calvinist; but in consequence of his misconduct and of being unhappily a fugitive in a foreign country, without money or friends, he was induced to change his religion for the sake of subsistence. To this end he procured admittance into a *hospice* for catechumens, that is to say, a house established for the reception of proselytes. The instructions he here received concerning some controversial points excited doubts he had not before entertained, and first caused him to realize the evil of the step he had taken. He was taught strange dogmas, and was eye-witness to stranger manners; and to these he saw himself a destined victim. He now sought to make his escape, but was prevented and more closely confined. If he complained, he was punished for complaining; and, lying at the mercy of his tyrannical oppressors, found himself treated as criminal because he could not without reluctance submit to be so.

Let those who are sensible how much the first acts of violence and injustice irritate young and inexperienced minds, judge of the situation of this unfortunate youth. Swollen with indignation, the tears of rage burst from his eyes. He implored the assistance of heaven and earth in vain; he appealed to the whole world, but no one attended to his plea. His complaints could reach the ears only of a number of servile domestics,—slaves to the wretch by whom he was thus treated, or accomplices in the same crime,—who ridiculed his non-conformity and endeavored to secure his imitation. He would doubtless have been entirely ruined had it not been for the good offices of an honest ecclesiastic, who came to the hospital on some business, and with whom he found an opportunity for a private conference. The good priest was himself poor, and stood in need of every one's assistance; the oppressed proselyte, however, stood yet in greater need of him. The former did not hesitate, therefore, to favor his escape, even at the risk of making a powerful enemy.

Having escaped from vice only to return to indigence, this young adventurer struggled against his destiny without success. For a moment, indeed, he thought himself above it, and at the first prospect of good fortune, his former distresses and his protector were forgotten together. He was soon punished, however, for his ingratitude, as his groundless hopes soon vanished. His youth stood in vain on his side; his romantic notions proving destructive to all his designs. Having neither capacity nor address to surmount the difficulties that fell in his way, and being a stranger to the virtues of moderation and the arts of knavery, he attempted so many things that he could bring none to perfection. Hence, having fallen into his former distress, and being not only in want of clothes and lodging, but even in danger of perishing with hunger, he recollected his former benefactor.

To him he returned, and was well received. The sight of the unhappy youth brought to the poor vicar's mind the remembrance of a good action;—a remembrance always grateful to an honest mind. This good priest was naturally humane and compassionate. His own misfortunes had taught him to feel for those of others, nor had prosperity hardened his heart. In a word, the maxims of true wisdom and conscious virtue had confirmed the kindness of his natural disposition. He cordially embraced the young wanderer, provided for him a lodging, and shared with him the slender means of his own subsistence. Nor was this all: he went still farther, freely giving him both instruction and consolation, and also endeavoring to teach him the difficult art of supporting adversity with patience. Could you believe, ye sons of prejudice! that a priest, and a priest in Italy too, could be capable of this?

This honest ecclesiastic was a poor Savoyard, who having in his younger days incurred the displeasure of his bishop, was obliged to pass the mountains in order to seek that provision which was denied him in his own country. He was neither deficient in literature nor understanding; his talents, therefore, joined with an engaging appearance, soon procured him a patron, who recommended him as tutor to a young man of quality. He preferred poverty, however, to dependence; and, being a stranger to the manners and behavior of the great, he remained but a short time in that situation. In quitting this service, however, he fortunately did not lose the esteem of his friend; and, as he behaved with great prudence and was universally beloved, he flattered himself that he should in time regain the good opinion of his bishop also, and be rewarded with some little benefice in the mountains, where he hoped to spend in tranquillity and peace the remainder of his days. This was the height of his ambition.

Interested by a natural affinity in favor of the young fugitive, he examined very carefully into his character and disposition. In this examination, he saw that his misfortunes had already debased his heart;—that the shame and contempt to which he had been exposed had depressed his ambition, and that his disappointed pride, converted into indignation, had deduced, from the injustice and cruelty of mankind, the depravity of human nature and the emptiness of virtue. He had observed religion made use of as a mask to self-interest, and its worship as a cloak to hypocrisy. He had seen the terms heaven and hell prostituted in the subtility of vain disputes; the joys of the one and the pains of the other being annexed to a mere repetition of words. He had observed the sublime and primitive idea of the Divinity disfigured by the fantastical imaginations of men; and, finding that in order to believe in God it was necessary to give up that understanding he hath bestowed on us, he held in the same disdain as well the sacred object of our idle reveries as those idle reveries themselves. Without knowing anything of natural causes, or giving himself any trouble to investigate them, he remained in a condition of the most stupid ignorance, mixed with profound contempt for those who pretended to greater knowledge than his own.

A neglect of all religious duties leads to a neglect of all moral obligations. The heart of this young vagabond had already made a great progress from one toward the other. Not that he was constitutionally vicious; but misfortune and incredulity, having stifled by degrees the propensities of his natural disposition, were hurrying him on to ruin, adding to the manners of a beggar the principles of an atheist.

His ruin, however, though almost inevitable, was not absolutely completed. His education not having been neglected, he was not without knowledge. He had not yet exceeded that happy term of life, wherein the youthful blood serves to stimulate the mind without inflaming the passions, which were as yet unrelaxed and unexcited. A natural modesty and timidity of disposition had hitherto supplied the place of restraint, and prolonged the term of youthful innocence. The odious example of brutal depravity, and of vices without temptation, so far from animating his imagination, had mortified it. Disgust had long supplied the place of virtue in the preservation of his innocence, and to corrupt this required more powerful seductions.

The good priest saw the danger and the remedy. The difficulties that appeared in the application did not deter him from the attempt. He took a pleasure in the design, and resolved to complete it by restoring to virtue the victim he had snatched from infamy.

To this end he set out resolutely in the execution of his project. The merit of the motive increased his hopes, and inspired means worthy of his zeal. Whatever might be the success, he was sure that he should not throw away his labor:—we are always sure so far to succeed in well doing.

He began with striving to gain the confidence of the proselyte by conferring on him his favors disinterestedly,—by never importuning him with exhortations, and by descending always to a level with his ideas and manner of thinking. It must have been an affecting sight to see a grave divine become the comrade of a young libertine—to see virtue affect the air of licentiousness —in order to triumph the more certainly over it. Whenever the heedless youth made him the confidant of his follies, and unbosomed himself freely to his benefactor, the good priest listened attentively to his stories; and, without approving the evil, interested himself in the consequences. No ill-timed censure ever indiscreetly checked the pupil's communicative temper. The pleasure with which he thought himself heard increased that which he took in telling all his secrets. Thus he was induced to make a free and general confession without thinking he was confessing anything.

Having thus made himself master of the youth's sentiments and character, the priest was enabled to see clearly that, without being ignorant for his years, he had forgotten almost everything of importance for him to know, and that the state of meanness into which he had fallen had almost stifled in him the sense of good and evil. There is a degree of low stupidity which deprives the soul as it were of life; the voice of conscience is also but little heard by those who think of nothing but the means of subsistence. To rescue this unfortunate youth from the moral death that so nearly threatened him, he began, therefore, by awakening his self-love and exciting in him a due regard for himself. He represented to his imagination a more happy success, from the future employment of his talents; he inspired him with a generous ardor by a recital of the commendable actions of others, and by raising his admiration of those who performed them. In order to detach him insensibly from an idle and vagabond life, he employed him in copying books; and under pretence of having occasion for such extracts, cherished in him the noble sentiment of gratitude for his benefactor. By this method he also instructed him indirectly by the books he employed him to copy; and induced him to entertain so good an opinion of himself as to think he was not absolutely good for nothing, and to hold himself not quite so despicable in his own esteem as he had formerly done.

A trifling circumstance may serve to show the art which this benevolent instructor made use of to insensibly elevate the heart of his disciple, without appearing to think of giving him instruction. This good ecclesiastic was so well known and esteemed for his probity and discernment, that many persons chose rather to entrust him with the distribution of their alms than the richer clergy of the cities. Now it happened that receiving one day a sum of money in charge for the poor, the young man had the meanness to desire some of it, under that title, for himself. " No," replied his kind benefactor, " you and I are brethren; you belong to me, and I should not apply the charity entrusted with me to my own use." He then gave him the desired sum from his private funds. Lessons of this kind are hardly ever thrown away on young people, whose hearts are not entirely corrupted.

But I will continue to speak no longer in the third person, which is indeed a superfluous caution; as you, my dear countrymen, are very sensible that the unhappy fugitive I have been speaking of is myself. I believe that I am now so far removed from the irregularities of my youth as to dare to avow them, and think that the hand which extricated me from them is too well deserving of my gratitude for me not to do it honour even at the expense of a little shame.

The most striking circumstance of all was to observe in the retired life of my worthy master virtue without hypocrisy and humanity without weakness. His conversation was always honest and simple, and his conduct ever conformable to his discourse. I never found him troubling himself whether the persons he assisted went constantly to vespers—whether they went frequently to confession—or fasted on certain days of the week. Nor did I ever know him to impose on them any of those conditions without which a man might perish from want, and have no hope of relief from the devout.

Encouraged by these observations, so far was I from affecting in his presence the forward zeal of a new proselyte, that I took no pains to conceal my thoughts, nor did I ever remark his being scandalized at this freedom. Hence, I have sometimes said to myself, he certainly overlooks my indifference for the new mode of worship I have embraced, in consideration of the disregard which he sees I have for that in which I was educated; as he finds my indifference is not partial to either. But what could I think when I heard him sometimes approve dogmas contrary to those of the Romish church, and appear to hold its ceremonies in little esteem? I should have been apt to consider him a protestant in disguise, had I seen him less observant of those very ceremonies which he seemed to think of so little account; but knowing that he acquitted himself as punctually of his duties as a priest in private as in public, I knew not how to judge of these seeming contradictions. If we except the failing which first brought him into disgrace with his superior, and of which he was not altogether corrected, his life was exemplary, his manners irreproachable, and his conversation prudent and sensible. As I lived with him in the greatest intimacy, I learned every day to respect him more and more; and as he had entirely won my heart by so many acts of kindness, I waited with an impatient curiosity to know the principles on which a life and conduct so singular and uniform could be founded.

It was some time, however, before this curiosity was satisfied, as he endeavored to cultivate those seeds of reason and goodness which he had endeavored to instill, before he would disclose himself to his disciple. The greatest difficulty he met with was to eradicate from my heart a proud misanthropy, a certain rancorous hatred which I bore to the wealthy and fortunate, as if they were made so at my expense, and had usurped apparent happiness from what should have been my own. The idle vanity of youth, which is opposed to all constraint and humiliation, encouraged but too much my propensity to indulge this splenetic humor; whilst that self-love, which my mentor strove so earnestly to cherish, by increasing my pride, rendered mankind, in my opinion, still more detestable, and only added to my hatred of them the most egregious contempt.

Without directly attacking this pride, he yet strove to prevent it from degenerating into barbarity, and without diminishing my self-esteem, made me less disdainful of my neighbors. In withdrawing the gaudy veil of external appearances, and presenting to my view the real evils it concealed, he taught me to lament the failings of my fellow creatures, to sympathize with their miseries, and to pity instead of envying them. Moved to compassion for human frailties from a deep sense of his own, he saw mankind everywhere the victims of either their own vices or of the vices of others,—he saw the poor groan beneath the yoke of the rich, and the rich beneath the tyranny of their own idle habits and prejudices.

"Believe me," said he, "our mistaken notions of things are so far from hiding our misfortunes from our view, that they augment those evils by rendering trifles of importance, and making us sensible of a thousand wants which we should never have known but for our prejudices. Peace of mind consists in a contempt for everything that may disturb it. The man who gives himself the greatest concern about life is he who enjoys it least; and he who aspires the most earnestly after happiness is always the one who is the most miserable."

"Alas!" cried I, with all the bitterness of discontent, "what a deplorable picture do you present of human life! If we may indulge ourselves in nothing, to what purpose were we born? If we must despise even happiness itself, who is there that can know what it is to be happy?"

"I know," replied the good priest, in a tone and manner that struck me.

"You!" said I, "so little favored by fortune! so poor! exiled! persecuted! can you be happy? And if you are, what have you done to purchase happiness?"

"My dear child," he replied, embracing me, "I will willingly tell you. As you have freely confessed to me, I will do the same to you. I will disclose to you all the sentiments of my heart. You shall see me, if not such as I really am, at least such as I believe myself to be: and when you have heard my whole *Profession of Faith*—when you know fully the situation of my heart—you will know why I think myself happy; and, if you agree with me, what course you should pursue in order to become so likewise.

"But this profession is not to be made in a moment. It will require some time to disclose to you my thoughts on the situation of mankind and on the real value of human life. We will therefore take a suitable opportunity for a few hours' uninterrupted conversation on this subject."

As I expressed an earnest desire for such an opportunity, an appointment was made for the next morning. We rose at the break of day and prepared for the journey. Leaving the town, he led me to the top of a hill, at the foot of which ran the river Po, watering in its course the fertile vales. That immense chain of mountains, called the Alps, terminated the distant view. The rising sun cast its welcome rays over the gilded plains, and, by projecting the long shadows of the trees, the houses, and adjacent hills, formed the most beautiful scene ever mortal eye beheld. One might have been almost tempted to think that nature had at this moment displayed all its grandeur and beauty as a subject for our conversation. Here it was that, after contemplating for a short time the surrounding objects in silence, my teacher and benefactor confided to me with impressive earnestness the principles and faith which governed his life and conduct.

PROFESSION OF FAITH OF A SAVOYARD VICAR

EXPECT from me neither learned declamations nor profound arguments. I am no great philosopher, and give myself but little trouble in regard to becoming such. Still I perceive sometimes the glimmering of good sense, and have always a regard for the truth. I will not enter into any disputation, or endeavor to refute you; but only lay down my own sentiments in simplicity of heart. Consult your own during this recital: this is all I require of you. If I am mistaken, it is undesignedly, which is sufficient to absolve me of all criminal error; and if I am right, reason, which is common to us both, shall decide. We are equally interested in listening to it, and why should not our views agree?

I was born a poor peasant, destined by my situation to the business of husbandry. It was thought, however, much more advisable for me to learn to get my bread by the profession of a priest, and means were found to give me a proper education. In this, most certainly, neither my parents nor I consulted what was really good, true, or useful for me to know; but only that I should learn what was necessary to my ordination. I learned, therefore, what was required of me to learn,—I said what was required of me to say—and, accordingly, was made a priest. It was not long, however, before I perceived too plainly that, in laying myself under an obligation to be no longer a man, I had engaged for more than I could possibly perform.

Some will tell us that conscience is founded merely on our prejudices, but I know from my own experience that its dictates constantly follow the order of nature, in contradiction to all human laws and institutions. We are in vain forbidden to do this thing or the other—we shall feel but little remorse for doing any thing to which a well-regulated natural instinct excites us, how strongly soever prohibited by reason. Nature, my dear youth, hath hitherto in this respect been silent in you. May you continue long in that happy state wherein her voice is the voice of innocence! Remember that you offend her more by anticipating her instructions than by refusing to hear them. In order to know when to listen to her without a crime, you should begin by learning to check her insinuations.

I had always a due respect for marriage as the first and most sacred institution of nature. Having given up my right to enter into such an engagement, I resolved, therefore, not to profane it: for, notwithstanding my manner of education, as I had always led a simple and uniform life, I had preserved all that clearness of understanding in which my first ideas were cultivated. The maxims of the world had not obscured my primitive notions, and my poverty kept me at a sufficient distance from those temptations that teach us the sophistry of vice.

The virtuous resolution I had formed, was, however, the very cause of my ruin, as my determination not to violate the rights of others, left my faults exposed to detection. To expiate the offence, I was suspended and banished; falling a sacrifice to my scruples rather than to my incontinence. From the reproaches made me on my disgrace, I found that the way to escape punishment for an offence is often by committing a greater.

A few instances of this kind go far with persons capable of reflection. Finding by sorrowful experience that the ideas I had formed of justice, honesty, and other moral obligations were contradicted in practice, I began to give up most of the opinions I had received, until at length the few which I retained being no longer sufficient to support themselves, I called in question the evidence on which they were established. Thus, knowing hardly what to think, I found myself at last reduced to your own situation of mind, with this difference only, that my unbelief being the later fruit of a maturer age, it was a work of greater difficulty to remove it.

I was in that state of doubt and uncertainty in which Descartes requires the mind to be involved, in order to enable it to investigate truth. This disposition of mind, however, is too disquieting to long continue, its duration being owing only to indolence or vice. My heart was not so corrupt as to seek fresh indulgence; and nothing preserves so well the habit of reflection as to be more content with ourselves than with our fortune.

I reflected, therefore, on the unhappy lot of mortals floating always on the ocean of human opinions, without compass or rudder—left to the mercy of their tempestuous passions, with no other guide than an inexperienced pilot, ignorant of his course, as well as from whence he came, and whither he is going. I often said to myself: I love the truth—I seek, yet cannot find it. Let any one show it to me and I will readily embrace it. Why doth it hide its charms from a heart formed to adore them?

I have frequently experienced at times much greater evils; and yet no part of my life was ever so constantly disagreeable to me as that interval of scruples and anxiety. Running perpetually from one doubt and uncertainty to another, all that I could deduce from my long and painful meditations was incertitude, obscurity, and contradiction; as well with regard to my existence as to my duty.

I cannot comprehend how any man can be sincerely a skeptic on principle. Such philosophers either do not exist, or they are certainly the most miserable of men. To be in doubt, about things which it is important for us to know, is a situation too perplexing for the human mind; it cannot long support such incertitude; but will, in spite of itself, determine one way or the other, rather deceiving itself than being content to believe nothing of the matter.

What added further to my perplexity was, that as the authority of the church in which I was educated was decisive, and tolerated not the slightest doubt, in rejecting one point, I thereby rejected in a manner all the others. The impossibility of admitting so many absurd decisions, threw doubt over those more reasonable. In being told I must believe all, I was prevented from believing anything, and I knew not what course to pursue.

In this situation I consulted the philosophers. I turned over their books, and examined their several opinions. I found them vain, dogmatical and dictatorial—even in their pretended skepticism. Ignorant of nothing, yet proving nothing; but ridiculing one another instead; and in this last particular only, in which they were all agreed, they seemed to be in the right. Affecting to triumph whenever they attacked their opponents, they lacked everything to make them capable of a vigorous defence. If you examine their reasons, you will find them calculated only to refute: If you number voices, every one is reduced to his own suffrage. They agree in nothing but in disputing, and to attend to these was certainly not the way to remove my uncertainty.

I conceived that the weakness of the human understanding was the first cause of the prodigious variety I found in their sentiments, and that pride was the second. We have no standard with which to measure this immense machine; we cannot calculate its various relations; we neither know the first cause nor the final effects; we are ignorant even of ourselves; we neither know our own nature nor principle of action; nay, we hardly know whether man be a simple or compound being. Impenetrable mysteries surround us on every side; they extend beyond the region of sense; we imagine ourselves possessed of understanding to penetrate them, and we have only imagination. Every one strikes out a way of his own across this imaginary world; but no one knows whether it will lead him to the point he aims at. We are yet desirous to penetrate, to know, everything. The only thing we know not is to contentedly remain ignorant of what it is impossible for us to know. We had much rather determine at random, and believe the thing which is not, than to confess that none of us is capable of seeing the thing that is. Being ourselves but a small part of that great whole, whose limits surpass our most extensive views, and concerning which its creator leaves us to make our idle conjectures, we are vain enough to decide what that whole is in itself, and what we are in relation to it.

But were the philosophers in a situation to discover the truth, which of them would be interested in so doing? Each knows very well that his system is no better founded than the systems of others; he defends it, nevertheless, because it is his own. There is not one of them, who, really knowing truth from falsehood, would not prefer the latter, if of his own invention, to the former, discovered by any one else. Where is the philosopher who would not readily deceive mankind, to increase his own reputation? Where is he who secretly proposes any other object than that of distinguishing himself from the rest of mankind? Provided he raises himself above the vulgar, and carries away the prize of fame from his competitors, what doth he require more? The most essential point is to think differently from the rest of the world. Among believers he is an atheist, and among atheists he affects to be a believer.

The first fruit I gathered from these meditations was to learn to confine my enquiries to those things in which I was immediately interested;—to remain contented in a profound ignorance of the rest; and not to trouble myself so far as even to doubt about what it did not concern me to know.

I could further see that instead of clearing up any unnecessary doubts, the philosophers only contributed to multiply those which most tormented me, and that they resolved absolutely none. I therefore applied to another guide, and said to myself, let me consult my innate instructor, who will deceive me less than I may be deceived by others; or at least the errors I fall into will be my own, and I shall grow less depraved in the pursuit of my own illusions, than in giving myself up to the deceptions of others.

Taking a retrospect, then, of the several opinions which had successively prevailed with me from my infancy, I found that, although none of them were so evident as to produce immediate conviction, they had nevertheless different degrees of probability, and that my innate sense of truth and falsehood leaned more or less to each. On this first observation, proceeding to compare impartially and without prejudice these different opinions with each other, I found that the first and most common was also the most simple and most rational; and that it wanted nothing more to secure universal suffrage, than the circumstance of having been last proposed. Let us suppose that all our philosophers, ancient and modern, had exhausted all their whimsical systems of power, chance, fate, necessity, atoms, an animated world, sensitive matter, materialism, and of every other kind; and after them let us imagine the celebrated Dr. Clarke enlightening the world by displaying the being of beings— the supreme and sovereign disposer of all things. With what universal admiration,— with what unanimous applause would not the world receive this new system,—so great, so consolatory, so sublime,—so proper to elevate the soul, to lay the foundations of virtue,—and at the same time so striking, so enlightened, so simple,—and, as it appears to me, pregnant with less incomprehensibilities and absurdities than all other systems whatever! I reflected that un- answerable objections might be made to all, because the human understanding is incapable of resolving them, no proof therefore could be brought exclusively of any: but what difference is there in proofs! Ought not that system then, which explains everything, to be preferred, when attended with no greater difficulties than the rest?

The love of truth then comprises all my philosophy; and my method of research being the simple and easy rule of common sense, which dispenses with the vain subtilty of argumentation, I reëxamined by this principle all the knowl- edge of which I was possessed, resolved to admit as evident everything to which I could not in the sincerity of my heart refuse to assent, to admit also as true all that seemed to have a necessary connection with it, and to leave everything else as uncertain, without either rejecting or admitting, being determined not to trouble myself about clearing up any point which did not tend to utility in practice.

But, after all, who am I? What right have I to judge of these things? And what is it that determines my con- clusions? If, subject to the impressions I receive, these are formed in direct consequence of those impressions, I trouble myself to no purpose in these investigations. It is necessary, therefore, to examine myself, to know what in- struments are made use of in such researches, and how far I may confide in their use.

In the first place, I know that I exist, and have senses whereby I am affected. This is a truth so striking that I am compelled to acquiesce in it. But have I properly a distinct sense of my existence, or do I only know it from my various sensations? This is my first doubt; which, at present, it is impossible for me to resolve: for, being continually affected by sensations, either directly from the objects or from the memory, how can I tell whether my self-consciousness be, or be not, something foreign to those sensations, and independent of them.

My sensations are all internal, as they make me sensible of my own existence; but the cause of them is external and independent, as they affect me without my consent, and do not depend on my will for their production or annihilation. I conceive very clearly, therefore, that the sensation which is internal, and its cause or object which is external, are not one and the same thing.

Thus I know that I not only exist, but that other beings exist as well as myself; to wit, the objects of my sensations; and though these objects should be nothing but ideas, it is very certain that these ideas are no part of myself.

Now, everything that I perceive out of myself, and which acts upon my senses, I call matter; and those portions of matter which I conceive are united in individual beings, I call bodies. Thus all the disputes between Idealists and Materialists signify nothing to me; their distinctions between the appearance and reality of bodies being chimerical.

Hence I have acquired as certain knowledge of the existence of the universe as of my own. I next reflect on the objects of my sensations; and, finding in myself the faculty of comparing them with each other, I perceive myself endowed with an active power with which I was before unacquainted.

To perceive is only to feel or be sensible of things; to compare them is to judge of their existence. To judge of things and to be sensible of them are very different. Things present themselves to our sensations as single and detached from each other, such as they barely exist in nature: but in our intellectual comparison of them they are removed, transported as it were, from place to place, disposed on and beside each other, to enable us to pronounce concerning their difference and similitude. The characteristic faculty

of an intelligent, active being is, in my opinion, that of
giving a sense to the word *exist*. In beings merely sensitive,
I have searched in vain to discover the like force of intel-
lect; nor can I conceive it to be in their nature. Such passive beings perceive every object singly or by itself; or if
two objects present themselves, they are perceived as united
into one. Such beings having no power to place one in com-
petition with, beside, or upon the other, they cannot compare
them, or judge of their separate existence.

To see two objects at once, is not to see their relations
to each other, nor to judge of their difference; as to see
many objects, though distinct from one another, is not to
reckon their number. I may possibly have in my mind the
ideas of a large stick and a small one, without comparing
those ideas together, or judging that one is less than the
other; as I may look at my hand without counting my
fingers.[1] The comparative ideas of greater and less, as well
as numerical ideas of one, two, etc., are certainly not sensations, although the understanding produces them only
from our sensations.

It has been pretended that sensitive beings distinguish
sensations one from the other, by the actual difference there
is between those sensations: this, however, demands an explanation. When such sensations are different, a sensitive
being is supposed to distinguish them by their difference;
but when they are alike, they can then only distinguish them
because they perceive one without the other; for, otherwise,
how can two objects exactly alike be distinguished in a
simultaneous sensation? Such objects must necessarily be
blended together and taken for one and the same; particularly according to that system of philosophy in which it is
pretended that the sensations, representative of extension,
are not extended.

When two comparative sensations are perceived, they
make both a joint and separate impression; but their relation to each other is not necessarily perceived in consequence
of either. If the judgment we form of this relation were
indeed a mere sensation, excited by the objects, we should

[1] M. de la Condamine tells of a people who knew how to reckon only as
far as three. Yet these people must often have seen their fingers without
ever having counted five.

never be deceived in it, for it can never be denied that I truly perceive what I feel.

How, therefore, can I be deceived in the relation between these two sticks, particularly, if they are not parallel? Why do I say, for instance, that the little one is a third part as long as the great one, when it is in reality only a fourth? Why is not the image, which is the sensation, conformable to its model, which is the object? It is because I am active when I judge, the operation which forms the comparison is defective, and my understanding, which judges of relations, mixes its errors with the truth of those sensations which are representative of objects.

Add to this the reflection, which I am certain you will think striking after duly weighing it, that if we were merely passive in the use of our senses, there would be no communication between them: so that it would be impossible for us to know that the body we touched with our hands and the object we saw with our eyes were one and the same. Either we should not be able to perceive external objects at all, or they would appear to exist as five perceptible substances of which we should have no method of ascertaining the identity.

Whatever name be given to that power of the mind which assembles and compares my sensations,—call it attention, meditation, reflection, or whatever you please,—certain it is that it exists in me, and not in the objects of those sensations. It is I alone who produce it, although it is displayed only in consequence of the impressions made on me by those objects. Without being so far master over myself as to perceive or not to perceive at pleasure, I am still more or less capable of making an examination into the objects perceived.

I am not, therefore, a mere sensitive and passive, but an active and intelligent being; and, whatever philosophers may pretend, lay claim to the honor of thinking. I know only that truth depends on the existence of things, and not on my understanding which judges of them; and that the less such judgment depends on me, the nearer I am certain of approaching the truth. Hence my rule of confiding more on sentiment than reason is confirmed by reason itself.

Being thus far assured of my own nature and capacity, I begin to consider the objects about me; regarding myself, with a kind of shuddering, as a creature thrown on the wide world of the universe, and as it were lost in an infinite variety of other beings, without knowing anything of what they are, either among themselves or with regard to me.

Everything that is perceptible to my senses is matter, and I deduce all the essential properties of matter from those sensible qualities, which cause it to be perceptible, and which are inseparable from it. I see it sometimes in motion and at other times at rest. This rest may be said to be only relative; but as we perceive degrees in motion, we can very clearly conceive one of the two extremes which is rest; and this we conceive so distinctly, that we are even induced to take that for absolute rest which is only relative. Now motion cannot be essential to matter, if matter can be conceived at rest. Hence I infer that neither motion nor rest are essential to it; but motion being an action, is clearly the effect of cause, of which rest is only the absence. When nothing acts on matter, it does not move; it is equally indifferent to motion and rest; its natural state, therefore, is to be at rest.

Again, I perceive in bodies two kinds of motion; that is a mechanical or communicated motion, and a spontaneous or voluntary one. In the first case, the moving cause is out of the body moved, and in the last, exists within it. I shall not hence conclude, however, that the motion of a watch, for example, is spontaneous; for if nothing should act upon it but the spring, that spring would not wind itself up again when once down. For the same reason, also, I should as little accede to the spontaneous motion of fluids, nor even to heat itself, the cause of their fluidity.

You will ask me if the motions of animals are spontaneous? I will freely answer, I cannot positively tell, but analogy speaks in the affirmative. You may ask me further, how I know there is such a thing as spontaneous motion? I answer, because I feel it. I *will* to move my arm, and, accordingly, it moves without the intervention of any other immediate cause. It is in vain to attempt to reason me out of this sentiment; it is more powerful than any rational evidence. You might as well attempt to convince me that I do not exist.

If the actions of men are not spontaneous, and there be no such spontaneous action in what passes on earth, we are only the more embarrassed to conceive what is the first cause of all motion. For my part I am so fully persuaded that the natural state of matter is a state of rest, and that it has in itself no principle of activity, that whenever I see a body in motion, I instantly conclude that it is either an animated body or that its motion is communicated to it. My understanding will by no means acquiesce in the notion that unorganized matter can move of itself, or be productive of any kind of action.

The visible universe, however, is composed of inanimate matter, which appears to have nothing in its composition of organization, or that sensation which is common to the parts of an animated body, as it is certain that we ourselves, being parts thereof, do not perceive our existence in the whole. The universe, also, is in motion; and its movements being all regular, uniform, and subjected to constant laws, nothing appears therein similar to that liberty which is remarkable in the spontaneous motion of men and animals. The world, therefore, is not a huge self-moving animal, but receives its motions from some foreign cause, which we do not perceive: but I am so strongly persuaded within myself of the existence of this cause, that it is impossible for me to observe the apparent diurnal revolution of the sun, without conceiving that some force must urge it forward; or if it is the earth itself that turns, I cannot but conceive that some hand must turn it.

If it be necessary to admit general laws that have no apparent relation to matter, from what fixed point must that enquiry set out? Those laws, being nothing real or substantial, have some prior foundation equally unknown and occult. Experience and observation have taught us the laws of motion; these laws, however, determine effects only without displaying their causes; and, therefore, are not sufficient to explain the system of the universe. Descartes could form a model of the heavens and earth with dice; but he could not give their motions to those dice, nor bring into play his centrifugal force without the assistance of a rotary motion. Newton discovered the law of attraction; but attraction alone would soon have reduced the universe into one solid mass: to this law, therefore, he found it necessary to add a projectile force, in order to account for the revolution of the heavenly bodies. Could Descartes tell us by what physical law his vortices were put and kept in motion? Could Newton produce the hand that first impelled the planets in the tangent of their respective orbits?

The first causes of motion do not exist in matter; bodies receive from and communicate motion to each other, but they cannot originally produce it. The more I observe the action and reaction of the powers of nature acting on each other, the more I am convinced that they are merely effects; and we must ever recur to some volition as the first cause: for to suppose there is a progression of causes to infinity, is to suppose there is no first cause at all. In a word, every motion that is not produced by some other, must be the effect of a spontaneous, voluntary act. Inanimate bodies have no action but motion; and there can be no real action without volition. Such is my first principle. I believe, therefore, that a *Will* gives motion to the universe, and animates all nature. This is my first article of faith.

In what manner volition is productive of physical and corporeal action I know not, but I experience within myself that it is productive of it. I *will* to act, and the action immediately follows; I *will* to move my body, and my body instantly moves; but, that an inanimate body lying at rest, should move itself, or produce motion, is incomprehensible and unprecedented. The *Will* also is known by its effects and not by its essence. I know it as the cause of motion; but to conceive matter producing motion, would be evidently to conceive an effect without a cause, or rather not to conceive any thing at all.

It is no more possible for me to conceive how the will moves the body, than how the sensations affect the soul. I even know not why one of these mysteries ever appeared more explicable than the other. For my own part, whether at the time I am active or passive, the means of union between the two substances appear to me absolutely incomprehensible. Is it not strange that the philosophers have thrown off this incomprehensibility, merely to confound the two substances together, as if operations so different could be better explained as the effects of one subject than of two.

The principle which I have here laid down, is undoubtedly something obscure; it is however intelligible, and contains nothing repugnant to reason or observation. Can we say as much of the doctrines of materialism? It is very certain that, if motion be essential to matter, it would be inseparable from it; it would be always the same in every portion of it, incommunicable, and incapable of increase or diminution; it would be impossible for us even to conceive matter at rest. Again, when I am told that motion is not indeed essential to matter, but necessary to its existence, I see through the attempt to impose on me by a form of words, which it would be more easy to refute, if more intelligible. For, whether the motion of matter arises from itself, and is therefore essential to it, or whether it is derived from some external cause, it is not further necessary to it than as the moving cause acting thereon: so that we still remain under the first difficulty.

General and abstract ideas form the source of our greatest errors. The jargon of metaphysics never discovered one truth; but it has filled philosophy with absurdities, of which we are ashamed as soon as they are stripped of their pompous expressions. Tell me truly, my friend, if any precise idea is conveyed to your understanding when you are told of a blind, unintelligent power being diffused throughout all nature? It is imagined that something is meant by those vague terms, Universal force and Necessary motion; and yet they convey no meaning. The idea of motion is nothing more than the idea of passing from one place to another, nor can there be any motion without some particular direction; for no individual being can move several ways at once. In what manner then is it that matter necessarily moves? Has all the matter of which bodies are composed a general and uniform motion, or has each atom a particular motion of its own? If we give assent to the first notion, the whole universe will appear to be one solid and indivisible mass; and according to the second, it should constitute a diffused and incoherent fluid, without a possibility that two atoms ever could be united. What can be the direction of this motion common to all matter? Is it in a right line upwards or downwards, to the right or to the left? Again, if every particle of matter has its particular direction, what can be the cause of all those directions and their variations? If every atom or particle of matter revolved only on its axis, none of them would change their place, and there would be no motion communicated; and even in this case it is necessary that such a revolving motion should be carried on one way. To ascribe to matter motion in the abstract, is to make use of terms without a meaning; and in giving it any determinate motion, we must of necessity suppose the cause that determines it. The more I multiply particular forces, the more new causes have I to explain, without ever finding one common agent that directs them. So far from being able to conceive any regularity or order in the fortuitous concourse of elements, I cannot even conceive the nature of their concurrence; and an universal chaos is more inconceivable than universal harmony. I easily comprehend that the mechanism of the world cannot be perfectly known to the human understanding, but whenever men undertake to explain it, they ought at least to speak in such a manner that others may understand them.

If from matter being put in motion I discover the existence of a *Will* as the first active cause, the subjugation of this matter to certain regular laws of motion displays also intelligence. This is my second article of faith. To act, to compare, to prefer, are the operations of an active, thinking being: such a being, therefore, exists. Do you proceed to ask me, where I discover its existence? I answer, not only in the revolutions of the celestial bodies; not only in myself; but in the flocks that feed on the plain, in the birds that fly in the air, in the stone that falls to the ground, and in the leaf that trembles in the wind.

I am enabled to judge of the physical order of things, although ignorant of their final cause; because to be able to form such a judgment it is sufficient for me to compare the several parts of the visible universe with each other, to study their mutual concurrence, their reciprocal relations, and to observe the general result of the whole. I am ignorant why the universe exists, but I am enabled nevertheless to see how it is modified. I cannot fail to perceive that intimate connection by which the several beings it is composed of afford each other mutual assistance. I resemble, in this respect, a man who sees the inside of a watch for the first time, and is captivated with the beauty of the work, although ignorant of its use. I know not, he may say, what this machine is good for, but I perceive that each part is made to fit some other. I admire the artist for every part of his performance, and am certain that all these wheels act thus in concert to some common end, which as yet I fail to comprehend.

But let us compare the partial and particular ends, the means whereby they are effected, and their constant relations of every kind; then let us appeal to our innate sense of conviction; and what man in his senses can refuse to acquiesce in such testimony? To what unprejudiced view does not the visible arrangement of the universe display the supreme intelligence of its author? How much sophistry does it not require to disavow the harmony of created beings, and that admirable order in which all the parts of the system concur to the preservation of each other? You may talk to me as much as you please of combinations and chances: what end will it answer to reduce me to silence, if you can persuade me into the truth of what you advance? and how will you divest me of that involuntary sentiment which continually contradicts you? If organized bodies are fortuitously combined in a thousand ways before they assume settled and constant forms; if at first they are formed stomachs without mouths, feet without heads, hands without arms, and imperfect organs of every kind, which have perished for want of the necessary faculties of self-preservation; how comes it that none of these imperfect essays have engaged our attention? Why hath nature at length confined herself to laws to which she was not at first subjected? I confess that I ought not to be surprised that any possible thing should happen, when the rarity of the event is compensated by the great odds that it did not happen. And yet

if any one were to tell me that a number of printer's types,
jumbled promiscuously together, had arranged themselves
in the order of the letters composing the Æneid, I certainly
should not deign to take one step to verify or disprove such
a story. It may be said, I forget the number of chances:
but pray how many must I suppose to render such a com-
bination in any degree probable? I, who see only the one,
must conclude that there is an infinite number against it,
and that it is not the effect of chance. Add to this that
the product of these combinations must be always of the
same nature with the combined elements; hence life and
organization never can result from a blind concourse of
atoms, nor will the chemist, with all his art in compounds,
ever find sensation and thought at the bottom of his cru-
cible.

I have been frequently surprised and sometimes scandalized in the reading of Nieuwentheit. What a presumption
was it to set down to make a book of those wonders
of nature that display the wisdom of their author? Had
his book been as big as the whole world, he would not have
exhausted his subject; and no sooner do we enter into the
minutiæ of things than the greatest wonder of all escapes
us;—that is, the harmony and connection of the whole.
The generation of living and organized bodies alone baffles
all the efforts of the human understanding. That insurmountable barrier which nature hath placed between the
various species of animals, that they might not be confounded with each other, makes her intentions sufficiently
evident. Not contented only to establish order, she has
taken effectual methods to prevent its being disturbed.

There is not a being in the universe which may not,
in some respect, be regarded as the common center of all
others, which are ranged around it in such a manner that
they serve reciprocally as cause and effect to one another.
The imagination is lost and the understanding confounded
in such an infinite diversity of relations, of which, however,
not one of them is either lost or confounded in the crowd.
How absurd the attempt to deduce this wonderful harmony
from the blind mechanism of a fortuitous jumble of atoms!
Those who deny the unity of design, so manifest in the

relation of all the parts of this grand system, may endeavor as much as they will to conceal their absurdities with abstract ideas, coördinations, general principles, and emblematical terms. Whatever they may advance, it is impossible for me to conceive that a system of beings can be so wisely regulated, without the existence of some intelligent cause which effects such regulation. It is not in my power to believe that passive inanimate matter could ever have produced living and sensible creatures,—that a blind fatality should be productive of intelligent beings,—or that a cause, incapable itself of thinking, should produce the faculty of thinking in its effects.

I believe, therefore, that the world is governed by a wise and powerful *Will*. I see it, or rather I feel it; and this is of importance for me to know. But is the world eternal, or is it created? Are things derived from one self-existent principle, or are there two or more, and what is their essence? Of all this I know nothing, nor do I see that it is necessary I should. In proportion as such knowledge may become interesting I will endeavor to acquire it: but further than this I give up all such idle disquisitions, which serve only to make me discontented with myself, which are useless in practice, and are above my understanding.

You will remember, however, that I am not dictating my sentiments to you, but only explaining what they are. Whether matter be eternal or only created, whether it have a passive principle or not, certain it is that the whole universe is one design, and sufficiently displays one intelligent agent: for I see no part of this system that is not under regulation, or that does not concur to one and the same end; viz. that of preserving the present and established order of things. That Being, whose will is his deed, whose principle of action is in himself,—that Being, in a word, whatever it be, that gives motion to all parts of the universe, and governs all things, I call God.

To this term I affix the ideas of intelligence, power, and will, which I have collected from the order of things; and to these I add that of goodness, which is a necessary consequence of their union. But I am not at all the wiser concerning the essence of the Being to which I give these attributes. He remains at an equal distance from my senses and my understanding. The more I think of him, the more I am confounded. I know of a certainty that he exists, and that his existence is independent of any of his creatures. I know also that my existence is dependent on his, and that every being I know is in the same situation as myself. I perceive the deity in all his works, I feel him within me, and behold him in every object around me: but I no sooner endeavor to contemplate what he is in himself,—I no sooner enquire where he is, and what is his substance, than he eludes the strongest efforts of my imagination; and my bewildered understanding is convinced of its own weakness.

For this reason I shall never take upon me to argue about the nature of God further than I am obliged to do by the relation he appears to stand in to myself. There is so great a temerity in such disquisitions that a wise man will never enter on them without trembling, and feeling fully assured of his incapacity to proceed far on so sublime a subject: for it is less injurious to entertain no ideas of the deity at all, than to harbor those which are unworthy and unjust.

After having discovered those of his attributes by which I am convinced of his existence, I return to myself and consider the place I occupy in that order of things, which is directed by him and subjected to my examination. Here I find my species stand incontestibly in the first rank; as man, by virtue of his will and the instruments he is possessed of to put it in execution, has a greater power over the bodies by which he is surrounded than they, by mere physical impulse, have over him. By virtue of his intelligence, I also find, he is the only created being here below that can take a general survey of the whole system. Is there one among them, except man, who knows how to observe all others?—to weigh, to calculate, to foresee their motions, their effects, and to join, if I may so express myself, the sentiment of a general existence to that of the individual? What is there so very ridiculous then in supposing every thing made for man, when he is the only created being who knows how to consider the relation in which all things stand to himself?

It is then true that man is lord of the creation,—that
he is, at least, sovereign over the habitable earth; for it is
certain that he not only subdues all other animals, and even
disposes by his industry of the elements at his pleasure, but
he alone of all terrestrial beings knows how to subject to
his convenience, and even by contemplation to appropriate
to his use, the very stars and planets he cannot approach.
Let any one produce me an animal of another species who
knows how to make use of fire, or hath faculties to admire
the sun. What! am I able to observe, to know other beings
and their relations,—am I capable of discovering what is
order, beauty, virtue,—of contemplating the universe,—of
elevating my ideas to the hand which governs the whole,—
am I capable of loving what is good and doing it, and shall I
compare myself to the brutes? Abject soul! it is your gloomy
philosophy alone that renders you at all like them. Or,
rather, it is in vain you would debase yourself. Your own
genius rises up against your principles;—your benevolent
heart gives the lie to your absurd doctrines,—and even the
abuse of your faculties demonstrates their excellence in
spite of yourself.

For my part, who have no system to maintain, who am
only a simple, honest man, attached to no party, unam-
bitious of being the founder of any sect, and contented with
the situation in which God hath placed me, I see nothing in
the world, except the deity, better than my own species; and
were I left to choose my place in the order of created beings,
I see none that I could prefer to that of man.

This reflection, however, is less vain than affecting; for my
state is not the effect of choice, and could not be due to the
merit of a being that did not before exist. Can I behold myself, nevertheless thus distinguished, without thinking myself happy in occupying so honorable a post; or without
blessing the hand that placed me here? From the first view
I thus took of myself, my heart began to glow with a sense
of gratitude towards the author of our being; and hence
arose my first idea of the worship due to a beneficent deity.
I adore the supreme power, and melt into tenderness at his
goodness. I have no need to be taught artificial forms of
worship; the dictates of nature are sufficient. Is it not a

natural consequence of self-love to honor those who protect us, and to love such as do us good?

But when I come afterwards to take a view of the particular rank and relation in which I stand, as an individual, among the fellow-creatures of my species; to consider the different ranks of society and the persons by whom they are filled; what a scene is presented to me! Where is that order and regularity before observed? The scenes of nature present to my view the most perfect harmony and proportion: those of mankind nothing but confusion and disorder. The physical elements of things act in concert with each other; the moral world alone is a chaos of discord. Mere animals are happy; but man, their lord and sovereign, is miserable! Where, Supreme Wisdom! are thy laws? Is it thus, O Providence! thou governest the world? What is become of thy power, thou Supreme Beneficence! when I behold evil thus prevailing upon the earth?

Would you believe, my good friend, that from such gloomy reflections and apparent contradictions, I should form to myself more sublime ideas of the soul than ever resulted from my former researches? In meditating on the nature of man, I conceived that I discovered two distinct principles; the one raising him to the study of eternal truth, the love of justice and moral beauty—bearing him aloft to the regions of the intellectual world, the contemplation of which yields the truest delight to the philosopher; the other debasing him even below himself, subjecting him to the slavery of sense, the tyranny of the passions, and exciting these to counteract every noble and generous sentiment inspired by the former. When I perceived myself hurried away by two such contrary powers, I naturally concluded that man is not one simple and individual substance. I will, and I will not; I perceive myself at once free, and a slave; I see what is good, I admire it, and yet I do the evil: I am active when I listen to my reason, and passive when hurried away by my passions; while my greatest uneasiness is to find, when fallen under temptations, that I had the power of resisting them.

Attend, young man, with confidence to what I say; you will find I shall never deceive you. If conscience be the offspring of our prejudices, I am doubtless in the wrong, and moral virtue is not to be demonstrated; but if self-love, which makes us prefer ourselves to every thing else, be natural to man, and if nevertheless an innate sense of justice be found in his heart, let those who imagine him to be a simple uncompounded being reconcile these contradictions, and I will give up my opinion and acknowledge him to be one substance.

You will please to observe that by the word substance I here mean, in general, a being possessed of some primitive quality, abstracted from all particular or secondary modifications. Now, if all known primitive qualities may be united in one and the same being, we have no need to admit of more than one substance; but if some of these qualities are incompatible with, and necessarily exclusive of each other, we must admit of the existence of as many different substances as there are such incompatible qualities. You will do well to reflect on this subject. For my part, notwithstanding what Mr. Locke hath said on this head, I need only to know that matter is extended and divisible, to be assured that it cannot think; and when a philosopher comes and tells me that trees and rocks have thought and perception, he may, perhaps, embarrass me with the subtlety of his arguments, but I cannot help regarding him as a disingenuous sophist, who had rather attribute sentiment to stocks and stones than acknowledge men to have a soul.

Let us suppose that a man, born deaf, should deny the reality of sounds, because his ears were never sensible of them. To convince him of his error, I place a violin before his eyes; and, by playing on another, concealed from him, give a vibration to the strings of the former. This motion, I tell him, is effected by sound.

"Not at all," says he, "the cause of the vibration of the string, is in the string itself: it is a common quality in all bodies so to vibrate."

"Show me then," I reply, "the same vibration in other bodies; or at least, the cause of it in this string."

"I cannot," the deaf man may reply, "but wherefore must I, because I do not conceive how this string vibrates, attribute the cause to your pretended sounds, of which I cannot entertain the least idea? This would be to attempt an explanation of one obscurity by another still greater. Either make your sounds perceptible to me, or I shall continue to doubt their existence."

The more I reflect on our capacity of thinking, and the nature of the human understanding, the greater is the resemblance I find between the arguments of our materialists and that of such a deaf man. They are, in effect, equally deaf to that internal voice which, nevertheless, calls to them so loud and emphatically. A mere machine is evidently incapable of thinking, it has neither motion nor figure productive of reflection: whereas in man there exists something perpetually prone to expand, and to burst the fetters by which it is confined. Space itself affords not bounds to the human mind: the whole universe is not extensive enough for man; his sentiments, his desires, his anxieties, and even his pride, take rise from a principle different from that body within which he perceives himself confined.

No material being can be self-active, and I perceive that I am so. It is in vain to dispute with me so clear a point. My own sentiment carries with it a stronger conviction than any reason which can ever be brought against it. I have a body on which other bodies act, and which acts reciprocally upon them. This reciprocal action is indubitable; but my will is independent of my senses. I can either consent to, or resist their impressions. I am either vanquished or victor, and perceive clearly within myself when I act according to my will, and when I submit to be governed by my passions. I have always the power to will, though not the force to execute it. When I give myself up to any temptation, I act from the impulse of external objects. When I reproach myself for my weakness in so doing, I listen only to the dictates of my will. I am a slave in my vices, and free in my repentance. The sentiment of my liberty is effaced only by my depravation, and when I prevent the voice of the soul from being heard in opposition to the laws of the body.

All the knowledge I have of volition, is deduced from a sense of my own; and, of the understanding, my knowledge is no greater. When I am asked what is the cause that determines my will, I ask in my turn, what is the cause that determines my judgment? for it is clear that these two

causes make but one: and if we conceive that man is active
in forming his judgment of things—that his understanding
is only a power of comparing and judging, we shall see that
his liberty is only a similar power, or one derived from
this—he chooses the good as he judges of the true, and for
the same reason as he deduces a false judgment, he makes
a bad choice. What then is the cause that determines his
will? It is his judgment. And what is the cause that determines his judgment? It is his intelligent faculty,—his
power of judging. The determining cause lies in himself.
If we proceed beyond this point, I know nothing of the
matter.

Not that I can suppose myself at liberty not to will my
own good, or to will my own evil: but my liberty consists in
this very circumstance, that I am incapable to will any thing
but what is useful to me, or at least what appears so, without
any foreign object interfering in my determination. Does
it follow from hence that I am not my own master because
I am incapable of assuming another being, or of divesting
myself of what is essential to my existence?

The principle of all action lies in the will of a free being.
We can go no farther in search of its source. It is not the
word liberty that has no signification; it is that of necessity.
To suppose any act or effect, which is not derived from an
active principle, is indeed to suppose effects without a cause.
Either there is no first impulse, or every first impulse can
have no prior cause; nor can there be any such thing as will
without liberty. Man is, therefore, a free agent, and as
such animated by an immaterial substance. This is my
third article of faith. From these three first you may easily
deduce all the rest, without my continuing to number them.

If man be an active and free being, he acts of himself.
None of his spontaneous actions, therefore, enter into the
general system of Providence, nor can be imputed to it.
Providence doth not contrive the evil, which is the consequence of man's abusing the liberty his creator gave him;
it only doth not prevent it, either because the evil which
so impotent a being is capable of doing is beneath its notice,
or because it cannot prevent it without laying a restraint
upon his liberty, and causing a greater evil by debasing his

nature. Providence hath left man at liberty, not that he should do evil, but good, by choice. It hath capacitated him to make such choice, in making a proper use of the faculties it hath bestowed on him. His powers, however, are at the same time so limited and confined, that the use he makes of his liberty is not of importance enough to disturb the general order of the universe. The evil done by man falls upon his own head, without making any change in the system of the world,—without hindering the human species from being preserved in spite of themselves. To complain, therefore, that God doth not prevent man from doing evil is, in fact, to complain that he hath given a superior excellence to human nature,—that he hath ennobled our actions by annexing to them the merit of virtue.

The highest enjoyment is that of being contented with ourselves. It is in order to deserve this contentment that we are placed here on earth and endowed with liberty,— that we are tempted by our passions, and restrained by conscience. What could Omnipotence itself do more in our favor? Could it have established a contradiction in our nature, or have allotted a reward for well-doing to a being incapable of doing ill? Is it necessary, in order to prevent man from being wicked, to reduce all his faculties to a simple instinct and make him a mere brute? No! never can I reproach the Deity for having given me a soul made in his own image, that I might be free, good, and happy like himself.

It is the abuse of our faculties which makes us wicked and miserable. Our cares, our anxieties, our griefs, are all owing to ourselves. Moral evil is incontestibly our own work, and physical evil would in fact be nothing, did not our vices render us sensible of it. Is it not for our preservation that nature makes us sensible of our wants? Is not pain of body an indication that the machine is out of order, and a caution for us to provide a remedy? And as to death, do not the wicked render both our lives and their own miserable? Who can be desirous of living here forever? Death is a remedy for all the evils we inflict on ourselves. Nature will not let us suffer perpetually. To how few evils are men subject who live in primeval sim-

plicity! They hardly know any disease, and are irritated
by scarcely any passions. They neither foresee death, nor
suffer by the apprehensions of it. When it approaches, their
miseries render it desirable, and it is to them no evil. If
we could be contented with being what we are, we should
have no inducement to lament our fate; but we inflict on
ourselves a thousand real evils in seeking after an imaginary
happiness. Those who are impatient under trifling incon-
veniences, must expect to suffer much greater. In our
endeavors to reëstablish by medicines a constitution impaired
by irregularities, we always add to the evil we feel, the
greater one which we fear. Our apprehensions of death
anticipate its horrors and hasten its approach. The faster
we endeavor to fly, the swifter it pursues us. Thus we are
terrified as long as we live, and die murmuring against
nature on account of those evils which we bring on ourselves
by doing outrage to her laws.

Enquire no longer then, who is the author of evil. Behold him in yourself. There exists no other evil in nature
than what you either do or suffer, and you are equally the
author of both. A general evil could exist only in disorder,
but in the system of nature I see an established order, which
is never disturbed. Particular evil exists only in the sentiment of the suffering being; and this sentiment is not given
to man by nature, but is of his own acquisition. Pain and
sorrow have but little hold on those who, unaccustomed
to reflection, have neither memory nor foresight. Take
away our fatal improvements—take away our errors and our
vices—take away, in short, every thing that is the work of
man, and all that remains is good.

Where every thing is good, nothing can be unjust, justice
being inseparable from goodness. Now goodness is the
necessary effect of infinite power and self-love essential
to every being conscious of its existence. An omnipotent
Being extends its existence also, if I may so express myself, with that of its creatures. Production and preservation follow from the constant exertion of its power: it does
not act on non-existence. God is not the God of the dead,
but of the living. He cannot be mischievous or wicked without hurting himself. A being capable of doing every thing

cannot ~~will to do any thing but~~ what is good. He who
is infinitely good, therefore, because he is infinitely powerful, must also be supremely just, otherwise he would be
inconsistent with himself. For that love of order which produces it we call goodness, and that love of order which preserves it is called justice.

God, it is said, owes nothing to his creatures. For my
part, I believe he owes them every thing he promised them
when he gave them being. Now what is less than to
promise them a blessing, if he gives them an idea of it, and
has so constituted them as to feel the want of it? The more
I look into myself, the more plainly I read these words
written in my soul: *Be just and thou wilt be happy.* I see
not the truth of this, however, in the present state of things,
wherein the wicked triumph and the just are trampled on
and oppressed. What indignation, hence, arises within us
to find that our hopes are frustrated! Conscience itself
rises up and complains of its maker. It cries out to him,
lamenting, *thou hast deceived me!*

"I have deceived thee! rash man? Who hath told thee
so? Is thy soul annihilated? Dost thou cease to exist?
Oh, Brutus! stain not a life of glory in the end. Leave not
thy honor and thy hopes with thy body in the fields of
Philippi. Wherefore dost thou say, virtue is a shadow,
when thou wilt yet enjoy the reward of thine own? Dost
thou imagine thou art going to die? No! thou art going
to live! and then will I make good every promise I have
made to thee."

One would be apt to think, from the murmurs of impatient mortals, that God owed them a recompense before
they had deserved it; and that he was obliged to reward
their virtue beforehand. No; let us first be virtuous, and
rest assured we shall sooner or later be happy. Let us not
require the prize before ~~we have won~~ the victory, nor de-
mand the price of our labor before the work be finished.
"It is not in the lists," says Plutarch, "that the victors at
our games are "crowned, but after the contests are over."

If the soul be immaterial, it may survive the body, and
if so, Providence is justified. Had I no other proof of the
immateriality of the soul, than the oppression of the just

and the triumph of the wicked in this world, this alone would prevent my having the least doubt of it. So shocking a discord amidst the general harmony of things, would make me naturally look out for the cause. I should say to myself, we do not cease to exist with this life,—every thing reassumes its order after death. I should, indeed, be embarrassed to tell where man was to be found, when all his perceptible properties were destroyed. At present, however, there appears to me no difficulty in this point, as I acknowledge the existence of two different substances. It is very plain that during my corporeal life, as I perceive nothing but by means of my senses, whatever is not submitted to their cognizance must escape me. When the union of the body and the soul is broken, I conceive that the one may be dissolved, and the other preserved entire. Why should the dissolution of the one necessarily bring on that of the other? On the contrary, being so different in their natures, their state of union is a state of violence, and when it is broken they both return to their natural situation. The active and living substance regains all the force it had employed in giving motion to the passive and dead substance to which it had been united. Alas! my failings make me but too sensible that man is but half alive in this life, and that the life of the soul commences at the death of the body.

But what is that life? Is the soul immortal in its own nature? My limited comprehension is incapable of conceiving any thing that is unlimited. Whatever we call infinite is beyond my conception. What can I deny, or affirm?—what arguments can I employ on a subject I cannot conceive? I believe that the soul survives the body so long as is necessary to justify Providence in the good order of things; but who knows that this will be forever? I can readily conceive how material bodies wear away and are destroyed by the separation of their parts, but I cannot conceive a like dissolution of a thinking being; and hence, as I cannot imagine how it can die, I presume it cannot die at all. This presumption, also, being consolatory and not unreasonable, why should I be fearful to indulge it?

I feel that I have a soul: I know it both from thought and sentiment: I know that it exists, without knowing its essence: I cannot reason, therefore, on ideas which I have not. One thing, indeed, I know very well, which is, that the identity of my being can be preserved only by the memory, and that to be in fact the same person, I must remember to have previously existed. Now I cannot recollect, after my death, what I was during life, without also recollecting my perceptions, and consequently my actions: and I doubt not but this remembrance will one day constitute the happiness of the just and the torment of the wicked. Here below, the violence of our passions absorbs the innate sentiment of right and wrong, and stifles remorse. The mortification and obloquy which virtue often suffers in the world, may prevent our being sensible of its charms. But when, delivered from the delusions of sense, we shall enjoy the contemplation of the Supreme Being, and those eternal truths of which he is the source;—when the beauty of the natural order of things shall strike all the faculties of the soul, and when we shall be employed solely in comparing what we have really done with what we ought to have done, then will the voice of conscience reassume its tone and strength; then will that pure delight, which arises from a consciousness of virtue, and the bitter regret of having debased ourselves by vice, determine the lot which is severally prepared for us. Ask me not, my good friend, if there may not be some other causes of future happiness and misery. I confess I am ignorant. These, however, which I conceive, are sufficient to console me under the inconveniencies of this life, and give me hopes of another. I do not pretend to say that the virtuous will receive any peculiar rewards; for what other advantage can a being, excellent in its own nature, expect than to exist in a manner agreeable to the excellence of its constitution? I dare affirm, nevertheless, that they will be happy: because their Creator, the author of all justice, having given them sensibility, cannot have made them to be miserable; and as they have not abused their liberty on earth, they have not perverted the design of their creation by their own fault: yet, as they have suffered evils in this life, they will certainly be indemnified in another. This opinion is not so much founded on the merits of a man, as on the notion of that goodness which appears to me inseparable from the divine nature. I only suppose the order of things strictly maintained, and that the Deity is ever consistent with himself.

It would be to as little purpose to ask me whether the torments of the wicked will be eternal. On this subject I am entirely ignorant, and have not the vain curiosity to perplex myself with such useless disquisitions. Indeed, why should I interest myself to discover their ultimate fate and destiny? I can never believe, however, that they will be condemned to everlasting torments.

If supreme justice avenges itself on the wicked, it avenges itself on them here below. It is you and your errors, ye nations! that are its ministers of vengeance. It employs the evils you bring on each other, to punish the crimes for which you deserve them. It is in the insatiable hearts of mankind,—corroding with envy, avarice, and ambition,— that their avenging passions punish them for their vices, amidst all the false appearances of prosperity. Where is the necessity of seeking a hell in another life, when it is to be found even in this,—in the hearts of the wicked.

Where our momentary necessities or senseless desires have an end, there ought our passions and our vices to end also. Of what perversity can pure spirits be susceptible? As they stand in need of nothing, to what end should they be vicious? If destitute of our grosser senses, can they be desirous of any thing but good? Doth not their happiness consist principally in contemplation, and is it possible that those who cease to be wicked should be eternally miserable?

This is what I am inclined to believe on this head, without giving myself the trouble to determine positively concerning the matter.

O righteous and merciful being! whatever be thy decrees, I acknowledge their rectitude. If thou punishest the wicked, my weak reason is dumb before thy justice. But if the remorse of those unfortunate wretches is to have an end,— if the same fate is one day to attend us all,—my soul exults in thy praise. Is not the wicked man, after all, my brother? How often have I been tempted to resemble him in partaking of his vices. O! may he be delivered from his misery;

may he cast off, also, that malignity which accompanies it; may he be ever as happy as myself; so far from exciting my jealousy, his happiness will only add to my own.

It is thus by contemplating God in his works, and studying him in those attributes which it imports me to know, that I learn by degrees to extend that imperfect and confined idea I had at first formed of the Supreme Being. But, if this idea becomes thus more grand and noble, it is proportionably less adapted to the weakness of the human understanding. In proportion as my mind approaches eternal light, its brightness dazzles and confounds me; so that I am forced to give up all those mean and earthly images which assist my imagination. God is no longer a corporeal and perceptible being: the supreme Intelligence which governs the world, is no longer the world itself; but in vain I endeavour to elevate my thoughts to a conception of his essence. When I reflect that it is he who gives life and activity to that living and active substance which moves and governs animated bodies,—when I am told that my soul is a spiritual being, and that God is also a spirit, I am incensed at this debasement of the divine essence, as if God and my soul were of the same nature, as if God was not the only absolute, the only truly active being,—perceiving, thinking and willing of himself,—from whom his creatures derive thought, activity, will, liberty, and existence. We are free only because it is his will that we should be so; his inexplicable substance being, with respect to our souls, such as our souls are in regard to our bodies. I know nothing of his having created matter, bodies, spirits, or the world. The idea of creation confounds me and surpasses my conception, though I believe as much of it as I am able to conceive. But I know that God hath formed the universe and all that exists, in the most consummate order. He is doubtless eternal, but I am incapacitated to conceive an idea of eternity. Why then should I amuse myself with words? All that I conceive is, that he existed before all things, that he exists with them, and will exist after them, if they should ever have an end. That a being, whose essence is inconceivable, should give existence to other beings, is at best obscure and incomprehensible to our ideas; but that something and nothing should be reciprocally converted into each other is a palpable contradiction, a most manifest absurdity.

God is intelligent; but in what manner? Man is intelligent by the act of reasoning, but the supreme intelligence lies under no necessity to reason. He requires neither premises nor consequences; nor even the simple form of a proposition. His knowledge is purely intuitive. He beholds equally what is and will be. All truths are to him as one idea, as all places are but one point, and all times one moment. Human power acts by the use of means, the divine power in and of itself. God is powerful because he is willing, his will constituting his power. God is good. Nothing is more manifest than this truth. Goodness in man, however, consists in a love to his fellow-creatures, and the goodness of God in a love of order; for it is on such order that the connexion and preservation of all things depend. Again, God is just. This I am fully convinced of, as justice is the natural consequence of goodness. The injustice of men is their own work, not his; and that moral disorder, which in the judgment of some philosophers makes against the system of providence, is in mine the strongest argument for it. Justice in man, indeed, is to render every one his due: but the justice of God requires at the hands of every one an account of the talents with which he has entrusted them.

In the discovery by the force of reason, however, of those divine attributes of which I have no absolute idea, I only affirm what I do not clearly comprehend; which is in effect to affirm nothing. I may say, it is true that, God is this or that; I may be sensible of it and fully convinced within myself, but I may yet be unable to conceive how, or in what manner he is so.

In short, the greater efforts I make to contemplate his infinite essence, the less I am able to conceive it. But I am certain that he is, and that is sufficient. The more he surpasses my conceptions, the more I adore him. I humble myself before him, and say:

"Being of beings! I am, because thou art. To meditate continually on thee is to elevate my thoughts to the fountain of existence. The most meritorious use of my reason is to be annihilated before thee. It is the delight of my soul, to feel my weak faculties overcome by the splendor of thy greatness."

After having thus deduced this most important truth, from the impressions of perceptible objects and that innate principle which leads me to judge of natural causes from experience, it remains for me to inquire what maxims I ought to draw therefrom for my conduct in life,—what rules I ought to prescribe to myself, in order to fulfill my destiny on earth agreeably to the design of him who placed me here. To pursue my own method, I deduce these rules, not from the sublime principles of philosophy, but find them written in indelible characters on my heart. I have only to consult myself concerning what I ought to do. All that I feel to be right, is right: whatever I feel to be wrong, is wrong. Conscience is the ablest of all casuists, and it is only when we are trafficking with her, that we have recourse to the subtilties of logical ratiocination. The chief of our concerns is that of ourselves; yet how often have we not been told by the monitor within, that to pursue our own interest at the expense of others would be to do wrong! We imagine, thus, that we are sometimes obeying the impulse of nature, and we are all the while resisting it. In listening to the voice of our senses we turn a deaf ear to the dictates of our hearts,—the active being obèys,—the passive being commands. Conscience is the voice of the soul,—the passions are the voice of the body. Is it surprising that these two voices should sometimes contradict each other, or can it be doubted, when they do, which ought to be obeyed? Reason deceives us but too often, and has given us a right to distrust her conclusions; but conscience never deceives us. She is to the soul what instinct[2] is to the body,—she is

---

[2] Modern philosophy, which affects to admit of nothing but what it can explain, hath nevertheless very unadvisedly admitted of that obscure faculty, called instinct, which appears to direct animals to the purposes of their being, without any acquisition of knowledge. Instinct, according to one of our greatest philosophers, is a habit destitute of reflection, but acquired by reflecting. Thus from the manner in which he explains its progress, we are led to conclude that children reflect more than grown persons; a paradox singular enough to require some examination. Without entering, however, into the discussion of it at present, I would only ask what name I am to give to that eagerness which my dog shows to pursue a mole, for instance, which he does not eat when he has caught it;—to that patience with which he stands watching for them whole hours, and to that expertness with which he makes them a prey the moment they reach the surface of the

man's truest and safest guide. Whoever puts himself under the conduct of this guide pursues the direct path of nature, and need not fear to be misled. This point is very important, (pursued my benefactor, perceiving I was going to interrupt him), permit me to detain you a little longer in order to clear it up.

All the morality of our actions lies in the judgments we ourselves form of them. If virtue be any thing real, it ought to be the same in our hearts as in our actions; and one of the first rewards of virtue is to be conscious of our putting it in practice. If moral goodness be agreeable to our nature, a man cannot be sound of mind or perfectly constituted, unless he be good. On the contrary, if it be not so and man is naturally wicked, he cannot become good without a corruption of his nature; goodness being contrary to his constitution. Formed for the destruction of his fellow-creatures, as the wolf is to devour its prey, an humane and compassionate man would be as depraved an animal as a meek and lamb-like wolf, while virtue only would leave behind it the stings of remorse.

Let us examine ourselves, my young friend, all partiality apart, and see which way our inclinations tend. Which is most agreeable to us, to contemplate the happiness or the miseries of others? Which is the most pleasing for us to do, and leaves the most agreeable reflection after it, an act of benevolence or of cruelty? For whom are we the most deeply interested at our theatres? Do you take a pleasure in acts of villainy? or do you shed tears at seeing the authors of them brought to condign punishment? It has been said that every thing is indifferent to us in which we are not

earth; and that in order only to kill them, without ever having been trained to mole hunting, or having been taught that moles were beneath the spot? I would ask further, as more important, why the first time I threaten the same dog, he throws himself down with his back to the ground and his feet raised in a suppliant attitude, the most proper of all others to excite my compassion; an attitude in which he would not long remain if I were so obdurate as to beat him lying in such a posture? Is it possible that a young puppy can have already acquired moral ideas? Can he have any notion of clemency and generosity? What experience can encourage him to hope he shall appease me, by giving himself up to my mercy? Almost all dogs do nearly the same thing in the same circumstances, nor do I advance any thing here of which every one may not convince himself. Let the philosophers, who reject so disdainfully the term instinct, explain this fact merely by the operation of our senses, and the knowledge thereby acquired; let them explain it, I say, in a manner satisfactory to any person of common sense, and I have no more to say in favor of instinct.

interested: the contrary, however, is certain; as the soothing endearments of friendship and humanity console us under affliction; and even in our pleasures we should be too solitary, too miserable, if we had nobody to partake them with us. If there be nothing moral in the heart of man, whence arise those transports of admiration and esteem we entertain for heroic actions and great minds? What has this virtuous enthusiasm to do with our private interest? Wherefore do I rather wish to be an expiring Cato, than a triumphant Cæsar? Deprive our hearts of a natural affection for the sublime and beautiful, and you déprive us of all the pleasures of life. The man whose meaner passions have stifled in his narrow soul such delightful sentiments,—he who by dint of concentrating all his affections within himself hath arrived at the pitch of having no regard for any one else, is no longer capable of such transports. His frozen heart never flutters with joy; no sympathetic tenderness brings the tears into his eyes; he is incapable of enjoyment. The unhappy wretch is void of sensibility: he is already dead.

But how great soever may be the number of the wicked, there are but few of these cadaverous souls—but few persons so insensible, if their own interest be set aside, to what is just and good. Iniquity never pleases unless we profit by it: in every other case it is natural for us to desire the protection of the innocent. When we see, for instance, in the street or on the highway, an act of injustice or violence committed, an emotion of resentment and indignation immediately rises in the heart, and incites us to stand up in defence of the injured and oppressed: but a more powerful consideration restrains us, and the laws deprive individuals of the right of taking upon themselves to avenge insulted innocence. On the contrary, if we happen to be witnesses to any act of compassion or generosity, with what admiration, with what esteem are we instantly inspired! Who is there that doth not, on such an occasion, say to himself, would that I had done as much! It is certainly of very little consequence to us whether a man was good or bad who lived two thousand years ago; and yet we are as much affected in this respect by the relations we meet with in ancient history, as if the transactions recorded had happened in our own times. Of what hurt is the wickedness of a Catiline to me? Am I afraid of falling a victim to his villainy? Wherefore, then, do I look upon him with the same horror as if he were my contemporary? We hate the wicked not only because their vices are hurtful, but also because they are wicked. We are not only desirous of happiness for ourselves, but also for the happiness of others; and when that happiness doth not diminish ours, it necessarily increases it. In a word, we cannot help sympathizing with the unfortunate, and always suffer when we are witnesses to their misery. The most perverse natures cannot be altogether divested of this sympathy; though it frequently causes them to act in contradiction to themselves. The robber who strips the passenger on the highway, will frequently distribute his spoils to cover the nakedness of the poor, and the most barbarous assassin may be induced humanely to support a man falling into a fit.

We hear daily of the cries of remorse for secret crimes, and frequently see remarkable instances of conscience bringing these crimes to light. Alas! who is a total stranger to this importunate voice? We speak of it from experience, and would be glad to silence so disagreeable a monitor. But let us be obedient to nature. We know that her government is very mild and gracious, and that nothing is more agreeable than the testimony of a good conscience, which ever follows our observance of her laws. The wicked man is afraid of, and shuns himself. He turns his eyes on every side in search of objects to amuse him. Without an opportunity for satire and raillery he would be always sad. His only pleasure lies in mockery and insult. On the contrary, the serenity of the just is internal. His smiles are not those of malignity but of joy. The source of them is found in himself, and he is as cheerful when alone as in the midst of an assembly. He derives not contentment from those who approach him, but communicates it to them.

Cast your eye over the several nations of the world: take a retrospective view of their various histories. Amidst all the many inhuman and absurd forms of worship,—amidst all that prodigious diversity of manners and characters,—

you will everywhere find the same ideas of justice and honesty,—the same notions of good and evil. Ancient paganism adopted the most abominable deities, which it would have punished on earth as infamous criminals—deities that presented no other picture of supreme happiness than the commission of crimes, and the gratification of their passions. But vice, armed even with sacred authority, descended in vain on earth. Moral instinct influenced the human heart to rebel against it. Even in celebrating the debaucheries of Jupiter, the world admired and respected the continence of *Xenocrates*. The chaste Lucretia adored the impudent Venus. The intrepid Roman sacrificed to Fear. They invoked the god Jupiter who disabled his father Saturn, and yet they died without murmuring by the hand of their own. The most contemptible divinities were adored by the noblest of men. The voice of nature, more powerful than that of the gods, made itself respected on earth, and seemed to have banished vice to heaven.

There evidently exists, then, in the soul of man, an innate principle of justice and goodness, by which, in spite of our own maxims, we approve or condemn the actions of ourselves and others. To this principle it is that I give the appellation of conscience.

At this word, however, I hear the clamor of our pretentious philosophers, who all exclaim about the mistakes of infancy and the prejudices of education. There is nothing, they say, in the human mind but what is instilled by experience; nor can we judge of anything but from the ideas we have acquired. Nay, they go farther, and venture to reject the universal sense of all nations; seeking some obscure example known only to themselves, to controvert this striking uniformity in the judgment of mankind: as if all the natural inclinations of the race were annihilated by the depravation of one people, and as if when monsters appeared the species itself were extinct. But what end did it serve to the skeptical Montaigne, to take so much trouble to discover in an obscure corner of the world a custom opposed to the common notions of justice? What end did it answer for him to place that confidence in the most suspicious travellers which he refused to the most celebrated writers? Should a few whimsical and uncertain customs, founded on local motives unknown to us, invalidate a general induction drawn from the united concurrence of all nations, contradicting each other in every other point and agreeing only in this? You pique yourself, Montaigne, on being ingenuous and sincere. Give us a proof, if it be in the power of a philosopher, of your frankness and veracity. Tell me if there be any country upon earth in which it is deemed a crime to be sincere, compassionate, beneficent, and generous, —in which an honest man is despicable, and knavery held in esteem?

It is pretended that every one contributes to the public good for his own interest; but whence comes it that the virtuous man contributes to it to his prejudice? Can a man lay down his life for his own interest? It is certain all our actions are influenced by a view to our own good; but unless we take moral good into the account, none but the actions of the wicked can ever be explained by motives of private interest. We imagine, indeed, that no more will be attempted; as that would be too abominable a kind of philosophy, by which we should be puzzled to account for virtuous actions; or could extricate ourselves out of the difficulty only by attributing them to base designs and sinister views;— by debasing a Socrates and calumniating a Regulus. If ever such doctrines should take rise among us, the voice of nature as well as of reason would check their growth and leave not even one of those who inculcate them the simple excuse of being sincere.

It is not my design here to enter into such metaphysical investigations, as surpass both your capacity and mine, and which in fact are useless. I have already told you I would not talk philosophy to you, but only assist you to consult your own heart. Were all the philosophers in Europe to prove me in the wrong, yet if you were sensible I was in the right, I should desire nothing more.

To this end you need only to distinguish between our acquired ideas and our natural sentiments, for we are sensible before we are intelligent; and as we do not learn to desire our own good and to avoid what is evil, but possess this desire immediately from nature, so the love of virtue and hatred of vice are as natural as the love of ourselves. The operations of conscience are not intellectual, but sentimental; for though all our ideas are acquired from without, the sentiments which estimate them arise from within; and it is by these alone that we know the agreement or disagreement which exists between us and those things which we ought to seek or shun.

To exist is, with us, to be sensible. Our sensibility is incontestably prior to our intelligence, and we were possessed of sentiment before we formed ideas. Whatever was the cause of our being, it hath provided for our preservation in furnishing us with sentiments agreeable to our constitution, nor can it possibly be denied that these at least are innate.

These sentiments are, in the individual,—the love of himself, aversion to pain, dread of death, and the desire of happiness. But if, as it cannot be doubted, man is by nature a social being, or at least formed to become such, his sociability absolutely requires that he should be furnished with other innate sentiments relative to his species; for to consider only the physical wants of men, it would certainly be better for them to be dispersed than assembled.

Now it is from this moral system,—formed by its duplicate relation to himself and his fellow creatures, that the impulse of conscience arises. To know what is virtuous is not to love virtue. Man has no innate knowledge of virtue; but no sooner is it made known to him by reason, than conscience induces him to love and admire it. This is the innate sentiment I mean.

I cannot think it impossible therefore to explain, from natural consequences, the immediate principle of conscience independent of reason; and, though it were impossible, it is not at all necessary; since those who reject this principle (admitted, however, and acknowledged in general by all mankind) do not prove its non-existence, but content themselves with affirming it only. When we affirm that it doth exist, we stand at least on as good a footing as they, and have besides that internal testimony for us,—the voice of conscience deposing in behalf of itself. If the first glimmerings of the understanding dazzle our sight, and make objects appear at first obscure or confused, let us wait but a little while till our eyes recover themselves and gather strength, and we shall presently see, by the light of reason, those same objects to be such as nature first presented them: or rather, let us be more simple and less vain; let us confine ourselves to the sentiments we first discovered, as it is to these our well-regulated studies must always recur.

O Conscience! Conscience! thou divine instinct, thou certain guide of an ignorant and confined, though intelligent and free being;—thou infallible judge of good and evil, who makest man to resemble the Deity. In thee consist the excellence of our nature and the morality of our actions. Without thee I perceive nothing in myself that should elevate me above the brutes, except the melancholy privilege of wandering from error to error by the assistance of an ill-regulated understanding and undisciplined reason.

Thank heaven, we are delivered from this formidable apparatus of philosophy. We can be men without being sages. Without spending our days in the study of morality, we possess at a cheaper rate a more certain guide through the immense and perplexing labyrinth of human opinions. It is not enough, however, that such a guide exists,—it is necessary to know and follow her. If she speaks to all hearts, it may be said, how comes it that so few understand her? It is, alas! because she speaks to us in the language of nature, which every thing conspires to make us forget. Conscience is timid,—she loves peace and retirement. The world and its noises terrify her. The prejudices she has been compelled to give rise to are her most cruel enemies, before whom she is silent or avoids their presence. Their louder voice entirely overpowers her's, and prevents her being heard. Fanaticism counterfeits her nature, and dictates in her name the greatest of crimes. Thus, from being often rejected, she at length ceases to speak to us, and answers not our inquiries after being long held in contempt; it also costs us as much trouble to recall, as it did at first to banish her from our bosoms.

How often in my researches have I found myself fatigued from my indifference! How often hath uneasiness and disgust, poisoning my meditations, rendered them insupportable! My insensible heart was susceptible only of a luke-warm and languishing zeal for truth. I said to myself, why should I take the trouble to seek after things that have no existence? Virtue is a mere chimera, nor is there any thing desirable but the pleasures of sense. When a man hath once lost a taste for the pleasures of the mind, how difficult to recover it! How much more difficult it also is for one to acquire such a taste who never possessed it! If there be in the world a man so miserable as never in his life to have done an action the remembrance of which must make him satisfied with himself, that man must be ever incapable of such a taste; and for want of being able to perceive that goodness which is conformable to his nature, must of necessity remain wicked as he is, and eternally miserable. But can you believe there exists on earth a human creature so depraved as never to have given up his heart to the inclination of doing good? The temptation is so natural and seductive, that it is impossible always to resist it, and the remembrance of the pleasure it hath once given us is sufficient to commend it to us ever afterwards. Unhappily, this propensity is at first difficult to gratify. There are a thousand reasons for our not complying with the dictates of our hearts. The false prudence of the world confines our good inclinations to ourselves, and all our fortitude is necessary to cast off the yoke. To take a pleasure in virtue is the reward of having been virtuous, nor is this prize to be obtained till it be merited.

Nothing is more amiable than virtue, but we must possess it, in order to find it such. When we court at first its embraces, it assumes, like Proteus in the fable, a thousand terrifying forms, and displays at last its own only to those who are tenacious of their hold.

Wavering perpetually between my natural sentiments, tending to the general good of mankind, and my reason, confining everything to my own, I should have remained all my life in this continual dilemma, doing evil yet loving good, in constant contradiction with myself, had not new knowledge enlightened my heart; had not the truth, which determined my opinions, directed also my conduct and rendered me consistent.

It is in vain to attempt the establishmment of virtue on the foundation of reason alone. What solidity is there in such a base? Virtue, it is said, is the love of order; but can or ought this love of order to prevail over that of my own happiness? Let there be given me a clear and sufficient reason for my giving it the preference. This pretended principle is at the bottom only a mere play upon words; as I may as well say that vice also consists in the love of order taken in a different sense. There is some kind of moral order in every thing that has sentiment and intelligence. The difference is that a good being regulates himself according to the general order of things, and a wicked being regulates things agreeably to his own private interest: the latter makes himself the centre of all things, and the former measures his radius and disposes himself in the circumference. Here he is arranged, with respect to the common centre, as God, and with respect to all concentric circles, as his fellow creatures. If there be no God, the wicked man only reasons right—the good man is a mere fool.

O my child! may you be one day sensible how great a weight we are relieved from, when, having exhausted the vanity of human opinions and tasted of the bitterness of the passions, we see ourselves at last so near the path to wisdom,—the reward of our good actions, and the source of that happiness we had despaired of obtaining.

Every duty prescribed by the laws of nature, though almost effaced from my heart by the injustice of mankind, again revived at the name of that eternal justice which imposed them, and was a witness to my discharge of them. I see in myself nothing more than the work and instrument of a superior being desirous of and doing good, desirous also of effecting mine by the concurrence of my will to his own, and by my making a right use of my liberty. I acquiesce in the regularity and order he hath established, being certain of enjoying one day or other that order in myself, and of finding my happiness therein: for what can afford greater felicity than to perceive one's self making a part of a system where every thing is constructed aright? On every occasion of pain or sorrow I support them with patience, reflecting that they are transitory and that they are derived from a body that is detached from myself. If I do a good action in secret, I know that it is nevertheless seen, and make the consideration of another life the rule of my conduct in this. If I am ever dealt with unjustly I say to myself, that just Being, who governs all things, knows how to indemnify me. My corporeal necessities and the miseries inseparable from this mortal life, make the apprehensions of death more supportable. I have hence so many chains the less to break when I am obliged to quit this mortal scene.

For what reason my soul is thus subjected to the organs of sense and chained to a body which lays it under so much restraint, I know not, nor presume to enter into the decrees of the Almighty. But I may, without temerity, form a modest conjecture or two on this subject. I reflect that, if the mind of man had remained perfectly free and pure, what merit could he have pretended to in admiring and pursuing that order which he saw already established, and which he would lie under no temptation to disturb? It is true he would have been happy, but he could not have attained that most sublime degree of felicity—the glory of virtue and the testimony of a good conscience. We should in such a case have been no better than the angels, and without doubt a virtuous man will be one day much superior. Being united on earth to a mortal body by ties not less powerful than incomprehensible, the preservation of that body becomes the great concern of the soul, and makes its present apparent interests contrary to the general order of things, which it is nevertheless capable of seeing and admiring. It is in this situation that by making a good use of his liberty, it becomes at once his merit and his reward; and that he prepares for himself eternal happiness in combating his earthly passions, and preserving the primitive purity of his will.

But even supposing that in our present state of depravity our primitive propensities were such as they ought to be, yet if all our vices are derived from ourselves, why do we complain that we are subjected by them? Why do we impute to the Creator those evils which we bring on ourselves, and those enemies we arm against our own happiness? Ah! let us not spoil the man of nature, and he will always be virtuous without constraint, and happy without remorse.

The criminals who pretend they are compelled to sin, are as
false as they are wicked. Is it possible for them not to
see that the weakness they complain of is their own work;
that their first depravation was owing to their own will;
that by their willfully yielding at first to temptations, they
at length find them irresistible? It is true they now cannot help their being weak and wicked; but it is their fault
that they at first became so. How easily might men pre-
serve the mastery over themselves and their passions
even during life if, before their vicious habits are acquired, when the faculties of the mind are just beginning
to be displayed, they should employ themselves on those
objects which it is necessary for them to know in order to
judge of those which are unknown; if they were sincerely
desirous of acquiring knowledge, not with a view of making
a parade in the eyes of others, but in order to render themselves wise, good, and happy in the practice of their natural
duties! This study appears difficult because we only apply
to it after being already corrupted by vice, and made
slaves to our passions. We place our judgment and esteem
on objects before we arrive at the knowledge of good and
evil, and then referring every thing to that false standard,
we hold nothing in its due estimation.

The heart, at a certain age, while it is yet free, eager,
restless, and anxious for happiness, is ever seeking it with
an impatient and uncertain curiosity; when deceived by
the senses, it fixes on the shadow of it, and imagines it to
be found where it doth not exist. This illusion hath prevailed too long with me. I discovered it, alas! too late; and
have not been able entirely to remove it: no, it will remain
with me as long as this mortal body, which gave rise to it.
It may prove as seductive, however, as it will, it can no
longer deceive me. I know it for what it is, and even while
I am misled by it, despise it. So far from esteeming it an
object of happiness, I see it is an obstacle to it. Hence I
long for that moment when I shall shake off this incum-
brance of body and be myself, without inconsistency or par-
ticipation with matter, and shall depend on myself only to
be happy. In the mean time I make myself happy in this
life, because I hold the evils of life as trifling in themselves;

as almost foreign to my being; and conceive at the same time that all the real good which may thence be deduced depends on myself.

To anticipate as much as possible that desirable state of happiness, power and liberty, I exercise my mind in sublime contemplations. I meditate on the order of the universe, not indeed with a view to explain it by vain systems, but to admire it perpetually and to adore its all-wise Creator, whose features I trace in his workmanship. With him I am thus enabled to converse, and to exert my faculties in the contemplation of his divine essence. I am affected by his beneficence, I praise him for his mercies, but never so far forget myself as to pray. For what should I ask of him? That he should for my sake pervert the order of things, and work miracles in my favor? Shall I, who ought to love and admire above all things that order which is established by his wisdom and maintained by his providence, desire that such order should be broken for me? No! such a rash petition would rather merit punishment than acceptance. Nor can I pray to him for the power of acting aright: for why should I petition for what he hath already given me? Hath he not given me conscience to love virtue, reason to know what it is, and liberty to make it my choice? If I do evil, I have no excuse: I do it because I will. To desire him to change my will, is to require that of him which he requires of me. This would be to desire him to do my work, while I receive the reward. Not to be content with my situation in the order of things, is to desire to be no longer a man; it is to wish that things were otherwise constituted than they are,—to wish for evil and disorder. No, thou source of justice and truth, God! merciful and just! placing my confidence in thee, the chief desire of my heart is that thy will be done. By rendering my will conformable to thine, I act as thou dost,—I acquiesce in thy goodness, and conceive myself already a partaker of that supreme felicity which is its reward.

The only thing which, under a just diffidence of myself, I request of him, or rather expect from his justice, is that he will correct my errors when I go astray. To be sincere, however, I do not think my judgment infallible: such of my opinions as seem to be the best founded may, nevertheless, be false; for what man hath not his opinions, and how few are there who agree in every thing? It is to no purpose that the illusions by which I am misled arise from myself; it is he alone who can dissipate them. I have done every thing in my power to arrive at truth; but its source is elevated beyond my reach. If my faculties fail me, in what am I culpable? Is it not then necessary for truth to stoop to my capacity?

The good priest spoke with much earnestness: he was deeply moved, and I was also greatly affected. I imagined myself attending to the divine Orpheus singing his hymns and teaching mankind the worship of the gods. A number of objections, however, to what he had said, suggested themselves; though I did not urge one, as they were less solid than perplexing; and though not convinced, I was nevertheless persuaded he was in the right. In proportion as he spoke to me from the conviction of his own conscience, mine confirmed me in the truth of what he said.

The sentiments you have been delivering, said I to him, appear newer to me in what you confess yourself ignorant of, than in what you profess to believe. I see in the latter a resemblance to that theism or natural religion which Christians affect to confound with atheism and impiety, though in fact diametrically opposite. In the present condition of my mind I find it difficult to adopt precisely your opinions and to be as wise as you. To be at least as sincere, however, I will consult my own conscience on these points. It is that internal sentiment which, according to your example, ought to be my monitor; and you have yourself taught me that, after having imposed silence on it for a long time, it is not to be awakened again in a moment. I will treasure up your discourse in my heart and meditate thereon. If I am as much convinced as you are, after I have duly weighed it, I will trust you as my apostle and will be your proselyte till death. Go on, however, to instruct me. You have only informed me of half I ought to know. Give me your thoughts on revelation, the scriptures, and those mysterious doctrines concerning which I have been in the dark from my infancy, without being able to conceive or believe them, and yet not knowing how to either admit or reject them.

Yes, my dear child, (said he), I will proceed to tell you what I think further. I meant not to open my heart to you by halves: but the desire which you express to be informed in these particulars, was necessary to authorize me to be totally without reserve. I have hitherto told you nothing but what I thought might be useful to you, and in the truth of which I am most firmly persuaded. The examination which I am now going to make is very different; presenting to my view nothing but perplexity, mysteriousness, and obscurity. I enter on it, therefore, with distrust and uncertainty. I almost tremble to determine about any thing, and shall, therefore, rather inform you of my doubts than of my opinions. Were your own sentiments more confirmed, I should hesitate to acquaint you with mine; but in your present skeptical situation, you will be a gainer by thinking as I do. Let my discourse, however, carry with it no greater authority than that of reason, for I frankly confess myself ignorant as to whether I am in the right or wrong. It is difficult, indeed, in all discussions, not to assume sometimes an affirmative tone; but remember that all my affirmations, in treating these matters, are only so many rational doubts. I leave you to investigate the truth of them. On my part, I can only promise to be sincere.

You will find that my exposition treats of nothing more than natural religion. It is very strange that we should stand in need of any other! By what means can I find out such necessity? In what respect can I be culpable for serving God agreeably to the dictates of the understanding he hath given me, and the sentiments he hath implanted in my heart? What purity of morals, what system of faith useful to man, or honorable to his Creator, can I deduce from any positive doctrines, that I cannot deduce equally as well from a good use of my natural faculties? Let any one show me what can be added, either for the glory of God, the good of society, or my own advantage, to the obligations we are laid under by nature. Let him show me what virtue can be produced from any new worship, which is not also the consequence of mine. The most sublime ideas of the Deity are inculcated by reason alone. Take a view of the works of nature, listen to the voice within, and then tell me what God hath omitted to say to your sight, your conscience, your understanding? Where are the men who can tell us more of him than he thus tells us of himself? Their revelations only debase the Deity, in ascribing to him human passions. So far from giving us enlightened notions of the Supreme Being, their particular tenets, in my opinion, give us the most obscure and confused ideas. To the inconceivable mysteries by which the Deity is hid from our view, they add the most absurd contradictions. They serve to make man proud, persecuting, and cruel. Instead of establishing peace on earth, they bring fire and sword. I ask myself what good purpose all this contention serves, without being able to resolve the question. Artificial religion presents to my view only the wickedness and miseries of mankind.

I am told, indeed, that revelation is necessary to teach mankind the manner in which God should be served. As a proof of this, they bring the diversity of whimsical modes of worship which prevail in the world; and that without remarking that this very diversity arises from the practice of adopting revelations. Ever since men have taken it into their heads to make the Deity speak, every people make him speak in their own way, and say what they like best. Had they listened only to what the Deity hath said to their hearts, there would have been but one religion on earth.

It is necessary that the worship of God should be uniform; I would have it so: but is this a point so very important that the whole apparatus of divine power was necessary to establish it? Let us not confound the ceremonials of religion with religion itself. The worship of God demands that of the heart; and this, when it is sincere, is ever uniform. Men must entertain very ridiculous notions of the Deity, indeed, if they imagine he can interest himself in the gown or cassock of a priest,—in the order of words he pronounces, or in the gestures and genuflexions he makes at

the altar. Alas! my friend, where is the use of kneeling?
Stand as upright as you may, you will always be near
enough to the earth. God requires to be worshipped in
spirit and in truth. This is a duty incumbent on men
of all religions and countries. With regard to exterior
forms, if their uniformity be expedient for the sake of
peace and good order, it is merely an affair of government;
the administration of which surely requires not the aid
of revelation.

I did not set out at first with these reflections. Hurried
on by the prejudices of education, and by that dangerous
self-conceit which ever elates mankind above their sphere,
as I could not raise my feeble conceptions to the Supreme
Being, I foolishly endeavored to debase him to my ideas.
Thus I connected relations infinitely distant from each
other, comparing the incomprehensible nature of the deity
with my own. I required still further a more immediate
communication with the Divinity, and more particular instructions concerning his will. Not content with reducing God
to a similitude with man, I wanted to be further distinguished by his favor, and to enjoy supernatural lights.
I longed for an exclusive and peculiar privilege of adora-
tion, and that God should have revealed to me what he had
kept secret from others, or that others should not understand
his revelations so well as myself.

Looking on the point at which I had arrived,—at that
whence all believers set out in order to reach an enlightened
mode of worship, I regarded natural religion only as the
elements of all religion. I took a survey of that variety of
sects which are scattered over the face of the earth, and
who mutually accuse each other of falsehood and error.
I asked which of them was right?

Every one of them in their turn answered *theirs.* I and
my partisans only think truly; all the rest are mistaken.

But, how do you know that your sect is in the right?
Because God hath declared so.

And who tells you that God hath so declared!
My spiritual guide, who knows it well. My pastor tells
me to believe so and so, and accordingly I believe it; he
assures me that every one who says to the contrary speaks

falsely; and, therefore, I listen to nobody who controverts his doctrine.[3]

How, thought I, is not the truth every where the same? Is it possible that what is true with one person can be false with another? If the method taken by him who is in the right, and by him who is in the wrong, be the same, what merit or demerit hath the one more than the other? Their choice is the effect of accident, and to impute it to them is unjust:—it is to reward or punish them for being born in this or that country. To say that the Deity can judge us in this manner is the highest impeachment of his justice.

Now, either all religions are good and agreeable to God, or if there be one which he hath dictated to man, and will punish him for rejecting, he hath certainly distinguished it by manifest signs and tokens as the only true one. These signs are common to all times and places, and are equally obvious to all mankind—to the young and old, the learned and ignorant, to Europeans, Indians, Africans, and Savages.

If there be only one religion in the world that can prevent our suffering eternal damnation, and there be on any part of the earth a single mortal who is sincere, and is not convinced by its evidence, the God of that religion must be the most iniquitous and cruel of tyrants. Would we seek the truth therefore in sincerity, we must lay no stress on the place or circumstance of our birth, nor on the authority of fathers and teachers; but appeal to the dictates of reason and conscience concerning every thing that is taught us in our youth. It is to no purpose to bid me subject my reason to the truth of things of which it is incapable of judging. The man who would impose on me a falsehood, may bid me do the same. It is necessary, therefore, I should employ my reason even to know when it ought to submit.

[3] All of them, says a certain wise and good priest, pretend that they derive their doctrines not from men, nor from any created being, but from God. But to say truth, without flattery or disguise, there is nothing in such pretentions: however they may talk, they owe their religion to human means. Witness the manner in which they first adopt it. The nation, country and place where they are born and bred determine it. Are we not circumcised or baptized,—made Jews, Turks, or Christians before we are men? Our religion is not the effect of choice; witness our lives and manners so little accordant to it; witness how we act contrary to the tenets of it on the most trifling occasions.—*Charron, on Wisdom.*

All the theology I am myself capable of acquiring, by taking a prospect of the universe and by the proper use of my faculties, is confined to what I have here laid down. To know more, we must have recourse to extraordinary means. These means cannot depend on the authority of men: for as all men are of the same species as myself, whatever another can by natural means come to the knowledge of, I can do the same; and another man is as liable to be deceived as I am. When I believe, therefore, what he says, it is not because he says it, but because he proves it. The testimony of mankind, therefore, is really that of my reason, and adds nothing to the natural means God hath given me for the discovery of the truth.

What then can even the apostle of truth have to tell me, of which I am not still to judge?

But God himself hath spoken; listen to the voice of revelation.

That, indeed, is another thing. God hath spoken! This is saying a great deal: but to whom hath he spoken?

He hath spoken to man.

How comes it then that I heard nothing of it?

He hath appointed others to teach you his word.

I understand you. There are certain men who are to tell me what God hath said. I had much rather have heard it from himself. This, had he so pleased, he could easily have done; and I should then have run no risk of deception. Will it be said I am secured from that by his manifesting the mission of his messengers by miracles? Where are those miracles to be seen? Are they related only in books? Pray, who wrote those books?

Men.

Who were witnesses to these miracles?

Men.

Always human testimony! It is always men who tell me what other men have told them. What a number of those are constantly between me and the Deity! We are always reduced to the necessity of examining, comparing, and verifying such evidence. O! that God had deigned to have saved me all this anxiety! Should I in that case have served him with a less willing heart?

Consider, my friend, in what a terrible discussion I am already engaged; what immense erudition I stand in need of to recur back to the earliest antiquity—to examine, to weigh, to confront prophecies, revelations, facts, with all the monuments of faith that have made their appearance in all the countries of the world; to ascertain their time, place, authors, and occasions. How great the critical sagacity which is requisite to enable me to distinguish between pieces that are suppositious, and those which are authentic; to compare objections with their replies, translations with their originals; to judge of the impartiality of witnesses, of their good sense, of their capacity; to know if nothing be suppressed or added to their testimony, if nothing be changed, transposed, or falsified; to obviate the contradictions that remain, to judge what weight we ought to ascribe to the silence of our opponents in regard to facts alleged against them; to discover whether such allegations were known to them; whether they did not disdain them too much to make any reply; whether books were common enough for ours to reach them; or, if we were honest enough to let them have free circulation among us, and to leave their strongest objections in full force.

Again, supposing that all these monuments of faith are acknowledged to be incontestable, we must proceed to examine the proofs of the mission of their authors. It would be necessary for us to be perfectly acquainted with the laws of chance and the doctrine of probabilities, to judge correctly what prediction could not be accomplished without a miracle; to know the genius of the original languages, in order to distinguish what is predictive in these languages and what is only figurative. It would be requisite for us to know what facts are agreeable to the established order of nature, and what are not so; to be able to say how far an artful man may not fascinate the eyes of the simple, and even astonish the most enlightened spectators; to know of what kind a miracle should be, and the authenticity it ought to bear, not only to claim our belief, but to make it criminal to doubt it; to compare the proofs of false and true miracles, and discover the certain means of dis-

tinguishing them; and after all to tell why the Deity should
choose, in order to confirm the truth of his word, to make
use of means which in their turn require confirmation, as
if he took delight in playing upon the credulity of mankind,
and had purposely avoided the direct means to persuade
them.

Suppose that the divine majesty hath really condescended
to make man the organ of promulgating its sacred will, is
it reasonable, is it just, to require all mankind to obey the
voice of such a minister, without his making himself known
to be such? Where is the equity or propriety in furnishing
him, for universal credentials, with only a few particular
tokens displayed before a handful of obscure persons, and
of which all the rest of mankind know nothing but by
hearsay? In every country in the world, if we should believe all the prodigies to be true which the common people
and the ignorant affirm to have seen, every sect would be
in the right; there would be more miraculous events than
natural ones; and the greatest miracle of all would be to
find that no miracles had happened where fanaticism had
been persecuted.

The Supreme Being is best displayed by the fixed and un-
alterable order of nature. If there should happen many
exceptions to such general laws, I should no longer know
what to think; and for my part, I must confess I believe
too much in God to believe in so many miracles so little
worthy of him.

What if a man should come and harangue us in the
following manner:

"I come, ye mortals, to announce to you the will of the
most high. Acknowledge in my voice that of him who sent
me. I command the sun to move backwards, the stars to
change their places, the mountains to disappear, the waves
to remain fixed on high, and the earth to wear a different
aspect."

Who would not, at the sight of such miracles, immediately
attribute them to the author of nature?

Nature is not obedient to impostors. Their miracles are
always performed in the highways, in the fields, or in apart-
ments where they are displayed before a small number of

spectators, previously disposed to believe every thing they see.

Who is there that will venture to decide how many eye-witnesses are necessary to render a miracle worthy of credit? If the miracles, intended to prove the truth of your doctrine, stand themselves in need of proof, of what use are they? Their performance might as well have been omitted.

The most important examination after all remains to be made into the truth of the doctrines delivered; for as those who say that God is pleased to work these miracles, pretend that the devil sometimes imitates them, we are no nearer a decision than before, though such miracles should be ever so well attested. As the magicians of Pharaoh worked the same miracles, even in the presence of Moses, as he himself performed by the express command of God, why might not they, in his absence, from the same proofs, pretend to the same authority? Thus after proving the truth of the doctrine by the miracle, you are reduced to the necessity of proving the truth of the miracle by that of the doctrine,[4] lest the works of the devil should be mistaken for those of the Lord. What think you of this alternative?

The doctrines coming from God, ought to bear the sacred characters of the divinity; and should not only clear up those confused ideas which unenlightened reason excites

[4] This is expressly mentioned in many places in scripture, particularly in Deuteronomy, chap. xiii., where it is said that, if a prophet, teaching the worship of strange Gods, confirm his discourse by signs and wonders, and what he foretells really comes to pass, so far from paying any regard to his mission, the people should stone him to death. When the Pagans, therefore, put the Apostles to death, for preaching up to them the worship of a strange God, proving their divine mission by prophesies and miracles, I see not what could be objected to them, which they might not with equal justice have retorted upon us. Now, what is to be done in this case? There is but one step to be taken, to recur to reason and leave miracles to themselves: better indeed had it been never to have had recourse to them, nor to have perplexed good sense with such a number of subtle distinctions. What! do I talk of subtle distinctions in christianity? If there are such, our Saviour was in the wrong surely to promise the Kingdom of Heaven to the weak and simple! How came he to begin his fine discourse on the Mount, with blessing the poor in spirit, if it requires so much ingenuity to comprehend and believe his doctrines? When you prove that I ought to subject my reason to his dictates, it is very well; but to prove that, you must render them intelligible to my understanding; you must adapt your arguments to the poverty of my genius, or I shall not acknowledge you to be the true disciple of your Master, or think that it is his doctrines which you would inculcate.

in the mind, but should also furnish us with a system of religion and morals agreeable to those attributes by which only we form a conception of his essence. If then they teach us any absurdities, if they inspire us with the sentiments of aversion for our fellow-creatures and fear for ourselves; if they describe the Deity as a vindictive, partial, jealous and angry being; as a God of war and of battles, always ready to thunder and destroy; always threatening slaughter and revenge, and even boasting of punishing the innocent, my heart cannot be incited to love so terrible a Deity, and I shall take care how I give up my natural religion to embrace such doctrines.

I should say to the advocates and professors of such a religion:

"Your God is not mine! A Being who began his dispensations with partiality, selecting one people and proscribing the rest of mankind, is not the common father of the human race; a Being who destines to eternal punishment the greater part of his creatures, is not that good and merciful God who is pointed out by my reason."

With regard to articles of faith, my reason tells me they should be clear, perspicuous, and evident. If natural religion be insufficient, it is owing to the obscurity in which it necessarily leaves those sublime truths it professes to teach. It is the business of revelation to exhibit them to the mind in a more clear and sensible manner; to adapt them to our understanding, and to enable us to conceive, in order that we may be capable of believing them. True faith is assured and confirmed by the understanding. The best of all religions is undoubtedly the clearest. That which is clouded with mysteries and contradictions, the worship that is to be taught me by preaching, teaches me by that very circumstance to distrust it. The God whom I adore is not a God of darkness; he hath not given me an understanding to forbid me the use of it. To bid me give up my reason, is to insult the author of it. The minister of truth doth not tyrannize over my understanding,—he enlightens it.

We have set aside all human authority, and without it, I cannot see how one man can convince another by preaching to him an unreasonable doctrine. Let us suppose two persons engaged in a dispute on this head, and see how they will express themselves in the language generally made use of on such occasions.

DOGMATIST.—Your reason tells you that the whole is greater than a part, but I tell you from God, that a part is greater than the whole.

RATIONALIST.—And who are you, that dare to tell me God contradicts himself? In whom shall I rather believe; in him who instructs me in the knowledge of eternal truths by means of reason, or in you who in his name would impose on me the greatest absurdities?

DOGMATIST.—In me, for my instructions are more positive, and I will prove to you incontestably that he hath sent me.

RATIONALIST.—How! will you prove that God hath sent you to depose against himself? What sort of proofs can you bring to convince me it is more certain that God speaks by your mouth, than by the understanding he hath given me?

DOGMATIST.—The understanding he hath given you! Ridiculous and contemptible man! You talk as if you were the first infidel who was ever misled by an understanding depraved by sin.

RATIONALIST.—Nor may you, man of God! be the first knave whose impudence hath been the only proof he could give of his divine mission.

DOGMATIST.—How! can Philosophers be thus abusive?

RATIONALIST.—Sometimes, when Saints set them the example.

DOGMATIST.—Oh! but I am authorized to abuse you. I speak on the part of God Almighty.

RATIONALIST.—It would not be improper, however, to produce your credentials before you assume your privileges.

DOGMATIST.—My credentials are sufficiently authenticated. Both heaven and earth are witnesses in my favor. Attend, I pray you, to my arguments.

RATIONALIST.—Arguments! why, you surely do not pretend to any! To tell me that my reason is fallacious, is to refute whatever it may say in your favor. Whoever refuses to abide by the dictates of reason, ought to be able to convince without making use of it. For, supposing that in the course of your arguments you should convince me, how shall I know whether it be not through the fallacy of reason depraved by sin, that I acquiesce in what you affirm? Besides, what proof, what demonstration, can you ever employ more evident than the axiom which destroys it? It is fully as credible that a just syllogism should be false, as that a part is greater than the whole.

DOGMATIST.—What a difference! My proofs admit of no reply; they are of a supernatural kind.

RATIONALIST.—Supernatural! What is the meaning of that term? I do not understand it?

DOGMATIST.—Contraventions of the order of nature; prophecies, miracles, and prodigies of every kind.

RATIONALIST.—Prodigies and miracles! I have never seen any of these things.

DOGMATIST.—No matter; others have seen them for you. We can bring clouds of witnesses—the testimony of whole nations—

RATIONALIST.—The testimony of whole nations! Is that a proof of the supernatural kind?

DOGMATIST.—No! But when it is unanimous it is incontestable.

RATIONALIST.—There is nothing more incontestable than the dictates of reason, nor can the testimony of all mankind prove the truth of an absurdity. Let us see some of your supernatural truths then, as the attestation of men is not so.

DOGMATIST.—Infidel wretch! It is plain that the grace of God doth not speak to thy understanding.

RATIONALIST.—Whose fault is that? Not mine; for, according to you, it is necessary to be enlightened by grace to know how to ask for it. Begin then, and speak to me in its stead.

DOGMATIST.—Is not this what I am doing? But you will not hear. What do you say to prophecies?

RATIONALIST.—As to prophecies; I say, in the first place, I have heard as few of them as I have seen miracles; and in the second, I say that no prophecy bears any weight with me.

DOGMATIST.—Thou disciple of Satan! And why have prophecies no weight with you?

RATIONALIST.—Because, to give them such weight requires three things, the concurrence of which is impossible. These are, that I should in the first place be a witness to the delivery of the prophecy; next, that I should be witness also to the event; lastly, that it should be clearly demonstrated to me that such event could not have occurred by accident. For, though a prophecy were as precise, clear, and determinate as an axiom of geometry, yet as the perspicuity of a prediction made at random does not render the accomplishment of it impossible, that accomplishment when it happens proves nothing in fact concerning the fore-knowledge of him who predicted it. You see, therefore, to what your pretended supernatural proofs, your miracles, and your prophecies reduce us:—to the folly of believing them all on the credit of others, and of submitting the authority of God speaking to our reason, to that of man. If those eternal truths, of which my understanding forms the strongest conception, can possibly be false, I can have no hope of ever arriving at certitude; and so far from being capable of being assured that you speak to me from God, I cannot even be assured of his existence.

You see, my child, how many difficulties must be removed before our disputants can agree; nor are these all. Among so many different religions, each of which proscribes and excludes the other, one only can be true; if, indeed, there be such a one among them all. Now, to discover which this is, it is not enough to examine that one; it is necessary to examine them all, as we should not, on any occasion whatever, condemn without a hearing. It is necessary to compare objections with proofs, and to know what each objects to in the others, as well as what the others have to say in their defence. The more clearly any sentiment or opinion appears demonstrated, the more narrowly it behooves us to inquire, what are the reasons which prevent its opponents from subscribing to it?

We must be very simple indeed, to think that an attention to the theologists of our own party sufficient to instruct us in what our adversaries have to offer. Where shall we find divines, of any persuasion, perfectly candid and honest? Do

they not all begin to weaken the arguments of their opponents before they proceed to refute them? Each is the
oracle of his party, and makes a great figure among his own
partisans, with such proofs as would expose him to ridicule
among those of a different persuasion.

Are you desirous of gaining information from books?
What a fund of erudition will not this require! How many
languages must you learn! How many libraries must you
turn over! And who is to direct you in the choice of the
books? There are hardly to be found in any one country
the best books on the contrary side of the question, and still
less is it to be expected that we should find books on all
sides. The writings of the adverse and absent party, were
they found also, would be very easily refuted. The absent
are always in the wrong; and the most weak and insufficient
arguments laid down with a confident assurance, easily efface
the most sensible and valid, when exposed with contempt.
Add to all this, that nothing is more fallacious than books,
nor exhibit less faithfully the sentiments of their writers.
The judgment which you formed, for instance, of the Roman
Catholic religion, from the treatise of Bossuet, was very
different from that which you acquired by residing among us.
You have seen that the doctrines we maintain in our contro-
versies with the Protestants, are not those which are taught
the common people; and that Bossuet's book by no means
resembles the instructions delivered from the pulpit.

To form a proper judgment of any religion, we are not to
deduce its tenets from the books of its professors; we must
go and learn it among the people. Each sect have their
peculiar traditions,—their customs, prejudices, and modes
of acceptation, which constitute the peculiar mode of their
faith. This should all be taken into consideration when we
form a judgment of their religion.

How many considerable nations are there who print no
books of their own, and read none of ours? How are they
to judge of our opinions, or we of theirs? We laugh at
them—they despise us; and though our travellers have turned
them into ridicule, they need only to travel among us, to
ridicule us in their turn. In what country are there not to
be found men of sense and sincerity, friends of humanity,

who require only to know truth, in order to embrace it? And yet every one imagines that truth is confined to his own particular system, and thinks that the religion of all other nations in the world is absurd. These foreign modes, therefore, cannot be in reality so very absurd as they appear, or the apparent reasonableness of ours is less real.

We have three principal religions in Europe. One admits only of one revelation, another of two, and the third of three. Each holds the other in detestation, anathematizes its possessors, accuses them of ignorance, obstinacy, and falsehood. What impartial person will presume to decide between them, without having first examined their proofs and heard their reasons? That which admits only of one revelation is the most ancient and seems the least disputable; that which admits of three is the most modern and seems to be the most consistent; that which admits of two and rejects the third, may possibly be the best, but it hath certainly every prepossession against it—its inconsistency stares one full in the face.

In all these three revelations, the sacred books are written in languages unknown to the people who believe in them. The Jews no longer understand Hebrew; the Christians neither Greek nor Hebrew; the Turks and Persians understand no Arabic, and even the modern Arabs themselves speak not the language of Mahomet. Is not this a very simple manner of instructing mankind, by talking to them always in a language which they do not comprehend? But these books, it will be said, are translated; a most unsatisfactory answer, indeed! Who can assure me that they are translated faithfully, or that it is even possible they should be so? Who can give me a sufficient reason why God, when he hath a mind to speak to mankind, should stand in need of an interpreter?

I can never conceive that what every man is indispensably obliged to know can be shut up in these books; or that he who is incapacitated to understand them, or the persons who explain them, will be punished for involuntary ignorance. But we are always plaguing ourselves with books. What a frenzy! Because Europe is full of books, the Europeans conceive them to be indispensable, without reflecting that

three-fourths of the world know nothing at all about them.
Are not all books written by men? How greatly, therefore,
must man have stood in need of them, to instruct him in his
duty, and by what means did he come to the knowledge of
such duties, before books were written? Either he must
have acquired such knowledge of himself, or it must have
been totally dispensed with.

We, Roman Catholics, make a great noise about the
authority of the church: but what do we gain by it, if it
requires as many proofs to establish this authority as other
sects also require to establish their doctrines? The church
determines that the church has a right to determine. Is not
this a special proof of its authority? And yet, depart from
this, and we enter into endless discussions.

Do you know many Christians who have taken the pains
to examine carefully into what the Jews have alleged against
us? If there are a few who know something of them, it is
from what they have met with in the writings of Christians:
a very strange manner indeed of instructing themselves in
the arguments of their opponents! But what can be done?
If any one should dare to publish among us such books as
openly espouse the cause of Judaism, we should punish the
author, the editor, and the bookseller.[5] This policy is very
convenient, and very sure to make us always in the right.
We can refute at pleasure those who are afraid to speak.

Those among us, also, who have an opportunity to converse with the Jews, have but little advantage. These unhappy people know that they are at our mercy. The tyranny
we exercise over them, renders them justly timid and reserved. They know how far cruelty and injustice are com-
patible with Christian charity. What, therefore, can they
venture to say to us, without running the risk of incurring
the charge of blasphemy? Avarice inspires us with zeal,
and they are too rich not to be ever in the wrong. The most
sensible and learned among them are the most circumspect

[5] Among a thousand known instances, the following stands in no need of
comment: the Catholic divines of the sixteenth century having condemned
all the Jewish books without exception to be burnt, a learned and illustrious
theologue, who was consulted on that occasion, had very nearly involved
himself in ruin by being simply of the opinion that such of them might
be preserved as did not relate to Christianity, or treated of matters foreign to religion.

and reserved. We make a convert, perhaps, of some wretched
hireling, to calumniate his sect; we set a parcel of pitiful
brokers disputing, who give up the point merely to gratify
us; but while we triumph over the ignorance or meanness of
such wretched opponents, the learned among them smile in
contemptuous silence at our folly. But do you think that
in places where they might write and speak securely, we
should have so much the advantage of them? Among the
doctors of the Sorbonne, it is as clear as daylight, that the
predictions concerning the Messiah relate to Jesus Christ.
Among the Rabbins at Amsterdam, it is just as evident that
they have no relation whatever to him. I shall never believe
that I have acquired a sufficient acquaintance with the arguments of the Jews, till they compose a free and independent
State, and have their schools and universities, where they
may talk and dispute with freedom and impunity. Till then
we can never really know what arguments they have to offer.

At Constantinople, the Turks make known their reasons,
and we dare not publish ours. There it is our turn to submit. If the Turks require us to pay to Mahomet, in whom
we do not believe, the same respect which we require the
Jews to pay to Jesus Christ, in whom they believe as little,
can the Turks be in the wrong and we in the right? On
what principle of equity can we resolve that question in our
own favor?

Two-thirds of mankind are neither Jews, Christians, nor
Mahometans. How many millions of men, therefore, must
there be who never heard of Moses, of Jesus Christ, or of
Mahomet? Will this be denied? Will it be said that our
missionaries are dispersed over the face of the whole earth?
This, indeed, is easily affirmed; but are there any of them
in the interior parts of Africa, where no European hath ever
yet penetrated? Do they travel through the inland parts of
Tartary, or follow on horseback the wandering hordes, whom
no stranger ever approaches, and who, so far from having
heard of the Pope, hardly know any thing of their own
Grand Lama? Do our missionaries traverse the immense
continent of America, where there are whole nations still
ignorant that the people of another world have set foot on
theirs? Are there any missionaries in Japan, from whence

their ill-behavior hath banished them forever, and where the
fame of their predecessors is transmitted to succeeding
generations as that of artful knaves, who, under cover of a
religious zeal, wanted to make themselves gradually masters
of the empire? Do they penetrate into the harems of the
Asiatic princes, to preach the gospel to millions of wretched
slaves? What will become of these secluded women for
want of a missionary to preach to them this gospel? Must
every one of them go to hell for being a recluse?

But were it true that the gospel is preached in every part
of the earth, the difficulty is not removed. On the eve pre-
ceding the arrival of the first missionary in any country,
some one person of that country expired without hearing
the glad tidings. Now what must we do with this one person? If there be but a single individual in the whole universe, to whom the gospel of Christ is not made known, the
objection which presents itself on account of this one person,
is as cogent as if it included a fourth part of the human
race.

Again, supposing that the ministers of the gospel are
actually present and preaching in those distant nations, how
can they reasonably hope to be believed on their own word,
and expect that their hearers will not scrupulously require
a confirmation of what is taught? Might not any one of
them very reasonably say to these preachers:

" You tell me of a God who was born and put to death
nearly two thousand years ago, in another portion of the
world, and in I know not what obscure town; assuring me
that all those who do not believe in this mysterious tale are
damned.

" These are things too strange to be readily credited on
the sole authority of a man who is himself a perfect stranger.

" Why hath your God brought those events to pass, of which
he requires me to be instructed, at so great a distance? Is
it a crime to be ignorant of what passes at the antipodes?
Is it possible for me to divine that there existed in the other
hemisphere a people called Jews, and a city called Jerusalem?
I might as well be required to know what happens in the
moon.

" You are come, you say, to inform me; but why did you

not come soon enough to inform my father, or why do you damn that innocent man because he knew nothing of the matter? Must he be eternally punished for your delay; he who was so just, so benevolent, and so desirous of knowing the truth?

"Be honest, and suppose yourself in my place. Do you think that I can believe, upon your testimony alone, all these incredible things you tell me, or that I can reconcile so much injustice with the character of that just God, whom you pretend to make known?

"Let me first, I pray you, go and see this distant country where so many miracles have happened that are totally unknown here. Let me go and be well informed why the inhabitants of that Jerusalem you speak of presumed to treat God like a thief or a murderer.

"They did not, you will say, acknowledge his divinity. How then can I, who never have heard of him but from you?

"You add, that they were punished, dispersed, and led into captivity;—not one of them ever approaching their former city.

"Assuredly, they deserved all this: but its present inhabitants,—what say they of the unbelief and *Deicide* of their predecessors? Do they not deny it, and acknowledge the divinity of the sacred personage just as little as did its ancient inhabitants?

"What! in the same city in which your God was put to death, neither the ancient nor present inhabitants acknowledge his divinity! And yet you would have me believe it, who was born nearly two thousand years after the event, and two thousand leagues distant from the place!

"Do you not see that, before I can give credit to this book, which you call sacred and of which I comprehend nothing, I ought to be informed from others as to when and by whom it was written; how it hath been preserved and transmitted to you; what is said of it in the country where it originated; and what are the reasons of those who reject it, although they know as well as you every thing of which you have informed me? You must perceive, therefore, the necessity I am under of going first to Europe, then to Asia, and lastly into Palestine to investigate and examine this subject for myself, and that I must be an absolute idiot to even listen to you before I have completed this investigation."

Such a discourse as this appears to me not only very reasonable, but I affirm that every sensible man ought under such circumstances to speak in the same manner, and to send a missionary about his business, who should be in haste to instruct and baptize him before he had sufficiently verified the proofs of his mission.

Now, I maintain that there is no revelation against which the same objections might not be made, and that with even greater force than against Christianity. Hence it follows that if there be in the world but one true religion, and if every one is obliged to adopt it under pain of damnation, it is necessary to spend our lives in the study of all religions, —to visit the countries where they have been established, and examine and compare them with each other. No man is exempted from the principal duty of his species, and no one hath a right to confide in the judgment of another. The artisan who lives only by his industry, the husbandman who cannot read, the timid and delicate virgin, the feeble valetudinarian, all must, without exception, study, meditate, dispute, and travel the world over in search of truth. There would no longer be any settled inhabitants in a country, the face of the earth being covered with pilgrims going from place to place, at great trouble and expense, to verify, examine, and compare the several different systems and modes of worship to be met with in different countries.

We must in such a case bid adieu to the arts and sciences, to trade, and to all the civil occupations of life. Every other study must give place to that of religion; while the man who should enjoy the greatest share of health and strength, and make the best use of his time and reason for the longest term of years allotted to human life, would, in his extreme old age, be still perplexed and undecided; and it would be indeed wonderful if, after all his researches, he should be able to learn before his death what religion he ought to have believed and practiced during his life.

Do you endeavor to mitigate the severity of this method, and place as little confidence as possible in the authority of your fellow men? In so doing, however, you place in them the greatest confidence: for if the son of a Christian does right in adopting, without a scrupulous and impartial examination, the religion of his father, how can the son of a Turk do wrong in adopting in the same manner the religion of Mahomet? I defy all the persecutors in the world to answer this question in a manner satisfactory to any person of common sense. Nay, some of them, when hard pressed by such arguments, will sooner admit that God is unjust, and visits the sins of the fathers upon the children, than give up their cruel and persecuting principles. Others, indeed, strive to elude the force of these reasons by civilly sending an angel to instruct those who, under absolute ignorance, lived, nevertheless, good moral lives. A very pretty device, truly, is that of the angel! Not contented with subjecting us to this angelic hierarchy, they would reduce even the Diety himself to the necessity of employing it.

See, my son, to what absurdities we are led by pride, and the spirit of persecution,—by being puffed up with our own vanity, and conceiving that we possess a greater share of reason than the rest of mankind.

I call to witness that God of peace whom I adore, and whom I would make known to you, that my researches have been always sincere; but seeing that they were and always must be unsuccessful, and that I was launched out into a boundless ocean of perplexity, I returned the way I came, and confined my creed within the limits of my first notions. I could never believe that God required me, under pain of eternal damnation, to be so very learned; and, therefore, I shut up all my books.

The book of nature lies open to every eye. It is from this sublime and wonderful volume that I learn to serve and adore its Divine Author. No person is excusable for neglecting to read this book, as it is written in an universal language, intelligible to all mankind.

Had I been born on a desert island, or had never seen a human creature beside myself; had I never been informed of what had formerly happened in a certain corner of the world; I might yet have learned, by the exercise and cultivation of my reason, and by the proper use of those faculties

God hath given me, to know and to love him. I might hence have learned to love and admire his power and goodness, and to have properly discharged my duty here on earth. What can the knowledge of the learned teach me more?

With regard to revelation: could I reason better or were I better informed, I might be made sensible perhaps of its truth and of its utility to those who are so happy as to believe it. But if there are some proofs in its favor which I cannot invalidate, there appear also to me many objections against it which I cannot resolve. There are so many reasons both for and against its authority that, not knowing what to conclude, I neither admit nor reject it. I reject only the obligation of submitting to it, because this pretended obligation is incompatible with the justice of God, and that, so far from its removing the obstacles to salvation, it raises those which are insurmountable by the greater part of mankind. Except in this article, therefore, I remain respectfully in doubt concerning the scriptures. I have not the presumption to think myself infallible. More able persons may possibly determine in cases that to me appear undeterminable. I reason for myself, not for them. I neither censure nor imitate them. Their judgment may possibly be better than mine, but am I to blame that it is not mine?

I will confess to you further, that the majesty of the scriptures strikes me with admiration, as the purity of the gospel hath its influence on my heart. Peruse the works of our philosophers, enriched with all their pomp of diction: how mean, how contemptible are they, compared with the scriptures! Is it possible that a book at once so simple and sublime should be merely the work of man? Is it possible that the sacred personage, whose history it contains, should be himself a mere man? Do we find that he assumed the tone of an enthusiast or ambitious sectary? What purity, what sweetness in his manners! What an affecting gracefulness in his delivery! What sublimity in his maxims! What profound wisdom in his discourses! What presence of mind, what subtilty, what truth in his replies! How great the command over his passions! Where is the man, where the philosopher who could so live and so die, without weakness and without ostentation? When Plato described an imaginary good man[6] loaded with all the shame of guilt, yet meriting the highest reward of virtue, he describes exactly the character of Jesus. The resemblance was so striking that all the fathers perceived it. What prepossession, what blindness must it be to compare the son of Sophroniscus to the son of Mary? What an infinite disproportion is there between them! Socrates, dying without pain or ignominy, easily supported his character to the last; and if his death, however easy, had not crowned his life, it might have been doubted whether Socrates, with all his wisdom, was any thing more than a vain sophist. He invented, it is said, the theory of morals. Others, however, had already put them in practice; he had only to say what they had done, and reduce their examples to precepts. Aristides had been just, before Socrates defined justice. Leonidas gave up his life for his country before Socrates declared patriotism to be a duty. The Spartans were a sober people before Socrates recommended sobriety. Before he had even defined virtue, Greece abounded in virtuous men. But where could Jesus learn, among his compatriots, that pure and sublime morality of which he only hath given us both precept and example?[7] The greatest wisdom was made known amidst the most bigoted fanaticism; and the simplicity of the most heroic virtues did honor to the vilest people on the earth. The death of Socrates, peaceably philosophizing with his friends, appears the most agreeable form that could be desired;— that of Jesus, expiring in the midst of agonizing pains, abused, insulted, cursed by a whole nation, is the most horrible that could be feared. Socrates, in receiving the cup of poison, blessed indeed the weeping executioner who administered it; but Jesus, in the midst of excruciating tortures, prayed for his merciless tormentors. Yes, if the life and death of Socrates are those of a sage, the life and death of Jesus are those of a God.

Shall we suppose the evangelic history a mere fiction? Indeed, my friend, it bears not the marks of fiction. On the contrary, the history of Socrates, which nobody pre-

---

[6] De Rep. dial. 1.
[7] See in his discourse on the Mount the parallel he makes between the morality of Moses and his own. Matthew v. 21, &c.

sumes to doubt, is not so well attested as that of Jesus Christ. Such a supposition, in fact, only shifts the difficulty without removing it. It is more inconceivable that a number of persons should agree to write such a history than that one only should furnish the subject of it. The Jewish authors were incapable of the diction, and were strangers to the morality contained in the gospel,—the marks of whose truth are so striking and inimitable, that the inventor would be a more astonishing character than the hero. And yet, with all this, the same gospel abounds with incredible relations, with circumstances repugnant to reason, and which it is impossible for a man of sense either to conceive of or to admit. What is to be done amidst all these contradictions? Be modest and circumspect. Regard in silence what cannot be either disproved or comprehended, and humble thyself before the Supreme Being who alone knoweth the truth.

Such is the involuntary skepticism in which I remain. This skepticism, however, is not painful to me, because it extends not to any essential point of practice; and as my mind is firmly settled regarding the principles of my duty, I serve God in the sincerity of my heart. In the mean time, I seek not to know any thing more than what relates to my moral conduct; and as to those dogmas which have no influence over the behavior, and about which so many persons give themselves so much trouble, I am not at all solicitous. I look upon the various particular religions as so many salutary institutions, prescribing in different countries an uniform manner of public worship; and which may all have their respective reasons, peculiar to the climate, government, or laws of the people adopting them, or some other motive which renders the one preferable to the other according to the circumstance of time and place. I believe all that are established to be good when God is served in sincerity of heart. This service is all that is essential. He rejects not the homage of the sincere, under whatsoever form they present it. Being called to the service of the church, I comply, therefore, with a scrupulous exactness, to all the forms it prescribes in my duty, and should reproach myself for the least wilful neglect of them. After having lain under a long prohibition I obtained, through the interest of M. de Mellerade, a permission to re-assume the functions of the priesthood, to procure me a livelihood. I had been accustomed formerly to say mass with all that levity and carelessness with which we perform the most serious and important offices after having very often repeated them. Since I entertained my new principles, however, I celebrate it with greater veneration:—penetrated by reflecting on the majesty of the Supreme Being, and the insufficiency of the human mind that is so little able to form conceptions relative to its author, I consider that I offer up the prayers of a people under a prescribed form of worship, and therefore carefully observe all its rites. I recite carefully; and strive not to omit the least word or ceremony. Before going to communicate, I first recollect myself, in order to do it with all those dispositions that the church and the importance of the sacrament require. I endeavor on this occasion to silence the voice of reason before the Supreme Intelligence. I say to myself: who art thou, to presume to set bounds to omnipotence? I reverently pronounce the sacramental words, and annex to them all·the faith that depends on me. Whatever, therefore, be the truth with regard to that inconceivable mystery, I am not fearful of being charged at the day of judgment with profaning it in my heart.

Honored with the ministerial office, though of the lowest rank, I will never do or say any thing that may make me unworthy to fulfill its sacred functions. I will always inculcate virtue, exhort my auditors to pursue it, and as far as it is in my power, set them an example. It does not depend on me to make their religion amiable, nor to confine the articles of their faith to what is necessary for all to believe: but God forbid that I should ever preach up the cruel tenets of persecution,—that I should even induce them to hate their neighbors, or to consign others to damnation.[8] Were I, indeed, in a superior station, this reserve might incur censure; but I am too insignificant to have much to

---

[8] The duty of adopting and respecting the religion of our country does not extend to such tenets as are contrary to moral virtue; such as that of persecution. It is this horrible dogma which arms mankind inhumanly against each other, and renders them destructive to the human race. The distinction between political and theological toleration is puerile and ridiculous, as they are inseparable, so that one cannot be admitted without the other.

fear, and I can never fall lower than I am. But whatever may happen, I shall never blaspheme Divine Justice, nor lie against the Spirit of Truth.

I have long been ambitious of the honor of being a pastor. I am indeed still ambitious, though I have no longer any hopes of it. There is no character in the world, my good friend, which appears to me so desirable as that of a pastor. A good pastor is a minister of goodness, as a good magistrate is a minister of justice. A pastor can have no temptation to evil; and though he may not always have it in his power to do good himself, he is really doing his duty when soliciting it of others, and very often obtains it when he learns to make himself truly worthy of respect.

O that I enjoyed but some little benefice among the poor people in our mountains! How happy should I then feel! for I cannot but think that I should make my parishioners happy! I should never, indeed, make them rich, but I should cheerfully partake of their poverty. I would raise them above meanness and contempt,—more insupportable than indigence itself. I would induce them to love concord, and to cherish that equality which often banishes poverty, and always renders it more supportable. When they should see that I was no richer than themselves, and yet lived content, they would learn to console themselves under their lot, and to live contented also.

In the instructions I should give them, I should be less directed by the sense of the church than by that of the gospel; whose tenets are more simple, and whose morals are more sublime;—that teaches few religious forms and many deeds of charity.

Before I should teach them their duty, I should always endeavor to practice it myself, in order to let them see that I really thought as I spoke.

Had I any protestants in my neighborhood, or in my parish, I would make no distinction between them and my own flock, in every thing that regarded acts of Christian charity. I would endeavor to make them all love and regard each other as brethren—tolerating all religions, and peacefully enjoying their own.

Thus, my young friend, have I given you with my own lips a recital of my creed, such as the Supreme Being reads it in my heart. You are the first person to whom I have made this *Profession of Faith;* and you are the only one, probably, to whom I shall ever make it. * * * * If I were more positive in myself, I should have assumed a more positive and dogmatic air; but I am a man ignorant and subject to error. I have opened to you my heart without reserve. What I have thought certain, I have given you as such. My doubts I have declared as doubts; my opinions as opinions; and I have honestly given you my reasons for both. What can I do more? It remains now for you to judge. Be sincere with yourself. Whether men love or hate, admire or despise you, is of but little moment. Speak only what is true, do only what is right; for, after all, the object of greatest importance is to faithfully discharge our duty. Adopt only those of my sentiments which you believe are true, and reject all the others; and whatever religion you may ultimately embrace, remember that its real duties are independent of human institutions—that no religion upon earth can dispense with the sacred obligations of morality—that an upright heart is the temple of the Divinity—and that, in every country and in every sect, to love God above all things, and thy neighbor as thyself, is the substance and summary of the law—the end and aim of religious duty.

CPSIA information can be obtained
at www.ICGtesting.com
Printed in the USA
LVHW110515160119
604076LV00001B/37/P